Mastering
GOLF'S
Mental Game

ALSO BY DR. MICHAEL LARDON

*Finding Your Zone: Ten Core Lessons for
Achieving Peak Performance in Sports and Life*

Your Ultimate
Guide to Better
On-Course
Performance
and Lower
Scores

Mastering

GOLF'S

Mental Game

Dr. Michael T. Lardon
with Matthew Rudy

Foreword by Phil Mickelson

CROWN
ARCHETYPE
NEW YORK

Published in the United States by Crown Archetype, an imprint of the Crown Publishing Group, a division of Random House LLC, a Penguin Random House Company, New York.
www.crownpublishing.com

Crown Archetype and design is a registered trademark of Random House LLC.

Library of Congress Cataloging-in-Publication Data
Lardon, Michael.
Mastering golf's mental game: your ultimate guide to better on-course performance and lower scores / Dr. Michael T. Lardon with Matthew Rudy; foreword by Phil Mickelson.
pages cm
1. Golf—Psychological aspects. I. Rudy, Matthew. II. Title.
GV979.P75L37 2014
796.352019—dc23
2014021023

ISBN 978-0-553-41791-3
eBook ISBN 978-0-553-41792-0

Printed in the United States of America

Book design: Ellen Cipriano
Jacket design: Gabriel Levine
Jacket photography: Dan Thornberg/Shutterstock; V Stock LLC/Tetra Images/Corbis

10 9 8 7 6 5 4 3 2 1

First Edition

To my beautiful wife,
Nadine,
and my children,
Lexi,
Lindsay,
and Theo

Contents

Foreword

by Phil Mickelson

My first interaction with Doc Lardon didn't have anything to do with golf. Mike and my brother Tim had become friends through Mike's work helping the men's golf team Tim coached at the University of San Diego. My brother knew about Mike's table tennis skill, and he thought it would be good fun to set me up for a match with a player who was out of my league—and who happened to live nearby. We met at a small gym at the Bridges Golf Club, where a Ping-Pong table had been set up. Tim had asked Mike to come in and teach me a lesson, so to speak.

Mike showed me some pretty cool things that day, and we had a good laugh. I had a few Ping-Pong scores I wanted to settle out on tour, and clearly Mike was a good guy to know. He helped me with the high toss serve and gave me footwork advice while playing me sitting in a chair. I followed by offering to help him with his short game. It wasn't until later—after I had learned more about Mike's work with Olympic athletes, NFL and MLB players, and other professional golfers—that we started talking about golf and the mental approach I used for my game.

My goals every season are to play my best golf and win major championships, and I'm always willing to try something different if I think it will help me toward those goals. I've been extremely fortunate to be surrounded by terrific people with expertise in many aspects of the game. About two years ago I was frustrated because I wasn't getting the results that the work I had been putting in on my game should have produced. That's where Mike came in. He helped me find some intangibles that make good golf great golf. His ideas about scoring the execution of each shot and redefining goals were particularly helpful.

Coming so close to winning a U.S. Open is unfortunately something I had experienced before 2013, but Merion was especially tough. Mike helped me see that in spite of that very difficult finish, my game was in a great place and I was continuing to play better and better. I went to Muirfield with more confidence than I had going into previous British Opens. I played the Scottish Open the week before and won in a playoff, which confirmed many of things that we had talked about. Then I played some of my best golf to win the Claret Jug. It's one of the most satisfying victories of my career.

Doc Lardon's Mental Scorecard is a simple way to incorporate his best strategies into your game. It will help you create a system that allows you to organize and evaluate the way you think on the course and give you a game plan to improve. Give it a try. You'll think better and play with more confidence, which leads to better scores.

Rancho Santa Fe, California

Introduction

FOR THE BETTER part of thirty years, I've been fortunate to work with—and compete against—athletes at the pinnacle of their sport. As a practicing medical doctor and sport psychiatrist, my twin specialties are mood disorders and the science of human performance. I've helped hundreds of professional and Olympic athletes strengthen their mental focus and achieve more favorable results, and I've talked about it in medical journals, in magazine articles, and on CNN. In my own athletic career, I've competed at a national level in table tennis since the late 1970s. Outside of the sports world, I've helped businesspeople, politicians, and members of elite military units think more efficiently on the job—and learn techniques that help them prepare for when things go wrong.

Simply put, I help people under pressure think better.

I help them find "The Zone."

At the highest levels of human performance—whether we're talking about professional athletes, world-class musicians, or elite surgeons—mental skills are the ones that separate the very best from the merely "great." Mental skills are the ones that let the greatest use the physical skills they already have.

In my first book, the national bestseller *Finding Your Zone,* I described the concept of The Zone, how it works, and how it applies to peak performance in sports and in life. It's essentially a technical manual to performance-related functions of the human brain.

That book did very well, but it wasn't golf specific, and it didn't address what I believe to be the two main misconceptions about "performance coaching": that it's only useful for highly skilled athletes, and that true "treatments" can't be generalized in a way that will work for a wide variety of players.

There's no question that elite athletes get tremendous benefit from mental coaching. Helping Phil Mickelson process his heartbreaking loss at the 2013 U.S. Open and turn around and win the British Open a month later was certainly exciting for me, both professionally and personally. But what is even more exciting is that the mental playbook Phil has used over the last few years to improve his thought processes is something any golfer—with any handicap—can use to shoot better scores.

And that's the true power of *Mastering Golf's Mental Game*. There may not be enough time or talent left in the world to physically hit the ball like Phil Mickelson can, but you can use *Mastering Golf's Mental Game* to develop a simple, powerful system for improving the way you think. It's a step-by-step how-to guide to thinking better on the golf course. It works for anyone—from a tour player to a 25-handicapper—and it answers the questions many of the other books in this genre either leave unanswered or cover in an overwhelming layer of science-speak. This isn't a pop psychology book and it isn't a medical journal. Instead of simplistically asking you to just think differently, I'm going to show you *how*, step by step, in straightforward, nontechnical language.

The methodology behind *Mastering Golf's Mental Game* came from an intense five-year period of work with more than two dozen golfers—prominent players like Phil, Lee Janzen, Rich Beem, and David Duval, and amateur players at different skill levels. Using the same techniques I had employed for my clients in other sports, I had seen some definite patterns emerge. As I watched these players practice and play over time—and as I recorded their feedback afterward—I found that anytime they hit a perfectly executed shot, they followed the exact same mental process from start to finish. This was consistent regardless of the player's individual circumstance or physical ability level—and whether it was conscious or unconscious.

As I drilled down to what this process entailed, I found the same six familiar psychological components kept coming up time and time again. These components work together in what I would eventually call the Pre-Shot Pyramid, and I began to build a series of simple, fun homework exercises to help refine the skills in each area—to build a more perfect Pyramid, so to speak.

The beauty of the Pyramid is twofold. First, the standard of "perfectly executed" is relative to a player's ability level. Perfectly executed means perfectly executed for you. For Phil Mickelson, that might mean hitting a 7-iron to three feet on the 17th hole on Sunday under full major championship pressure. For you, it might mean hitting a solid drive in the center of the fairway on the 1st hole with your three regular playing partners watching.

Second, and more importantly, this Pre-Shot Pyramid sequence is 100 percent learnable and repeatable no matter what your handicap level is. You don't have to be a superhuman athlete to do it.

Once I had a basic course map of the pieces at

work, I wanted to build a straightforward way to measure progress toward getting those pieces working together optimally. This presented a unique challenge: Ultimately, mental focus is about performing in the moment without any conscious thought about consequences or results, which is at odds with the whole idea of keeping score.

The measuring system I came up with integrated two scorecards into a player's routine. In addition to the standard card used to record score, I added a second scorecard designed to measure a player's progress perfecting the steps of the Pre-Shot Pyramid *on every shot*. It helps a player to concentrate on each individual shot as it happens—the essence of being in The Zone—rather than focus on the score at the end of the hole or the end of the round.

I spent five years perfecting and streamlining the Pre-Shot Pyramid concept and the two-scorecard measuring system, and by 2011, I was excited to show it off to someone outside of my familiar group of clients.

Phil Mickelson was the perfect focus group, so to speak.

That spring I was at his home course, the Bridges at Rancho Santa Fe, in Rancho Santa Fe, California, sitting on a bench in a secluded part of the practice area. Phil was going through one of his normal practice sessions about twelve feet in front of me.

When Phil stopped to take a break, I asked him to show me what his process was for a real shot in a tournament, from getting yardage from his caddie to pulling the club and going through his routine. After he hit a shot, I described the Pre-Shot Pyramid to him and went over the basics of the two-scorecard system. One of the reasons Phil has been so successful for so long is his complete lack of ego when it comes to incorporating new ideas into his game. He's a naturally open, curious person and he's extremely intelligent, and if he finds something he thinks can help him, he won't hesitate to use it—whether it's playing two drivers at Augusta National or experimenting with a belly putter after watching Keegan Bradley's success with it.

Phil listened closely to my description, and how it all worked, and said he'd give it a try. He paused for a few seconds to soak it up and then hit the next shot—a little wedge.

Right after he made contact, I reflexively asked him, "How was that?" I didn't have to see the answer. I heard it when the ball hit the flag. Picking a target 158 yards away and just under a little ridge, he alternated hitting cut 8-irons and high, drawing 9-irons. After twenty shots, a dozen of them were inside four feet from the hole.

I've spent many years around tour players, including several as a part-time caddie for my brother, Brad, who played five years on the PGA Tour. I've seen plenty of expert shot-making and thousands of great shots. But watching Phil was to see a true virtuoso—like a Mozart in the world of golf.

When he finished, Phil told me that he really liked—in his words—the "mental scorecard" part of the system, and he was going to try it out under tournament conditions. Coincidence or not, the next week he went out and won the Shell Houston Open. A name for my system was born, and it was the start of a terrific relationship with Phil.

In *Mastering Golf's Mental Game,* I'm going to show you the same process. In section one, we'll talk about the six basic building blocks of the Pre-Shot Pyramid— attitude, motivation, control, optimization, concentration, and planning—and how they piece together. I call these the Six Components of Mental Excellence, and they've been developed over decades of study, lab research, and fieldwork. Each chapter is filled with a variety of simple, fun exercises that will help you become a better player immediately, from the comfort of your living room. They're the actual exercises I use with my professional clients every day.

In the second section, we'll move on to the Mental Scorecard, where the theoretical components turn into real-world skills usable on the golf course. You'll learn how the Pre-Shot Pyramid comes together, how the Mental Scorecard works, and how to tune both perfectly for your brain and your game. The system I describe in the book is identical to the one I use with my professional clients, and it will give you the ultimate step-by-step prescription for a powerful, focused mental game—the key to shooting lower scores.

I encourage you to use this book as a true workbook: Highlight, make notes, and dip into the material at places you see fit. The Mental Scorecard section of the book is strong enough—and simple enough—that you could certainly skip the conceptual material in part one and get real benefits. But my experience with professional clients has shown that even a basic run-through of the concepts included in the first section produces both more and more consistent improvement when coupled with the scorecard itself.

Throughout the book, you'll find a variety of case studies illustrating the real-world pitfalls and possibilities of the Six Components of Mental Excellence. Case studies like these form the backbone of study in the best medical and business schools around the world, and they're extremely useful. I use case studies for two reasons. First, the details of the cases can be constructed so that they provide a terrific representation of the lesson I'm trying to teach. Second, I do it out of respect for my clients' privacy, when appropriate.

One of the unique credentials I bring to the world

of sport performance is my role as a practicing medi-cal doctor. My work with some clients goes far beyond an occasional phone call or motivational pep talk at the practice range before a round. I'm grateful to my clients for allowing me to share some of the details of our work together. In some cases you'll hear firsthand about the work I've done with real players, while in others I'll share a case built from a composite of sev-eral different clients I've observed. In both cases I'm sure you'll find them illuminating and instructive.

Taken as a whole, the Mental Scorecard system will transform the way you think about your game, and the way you play it. You'll play to your potential, get the most out of your talent, and—most importantly—enjoy it more than you ever have.

CHAPTER 1

The Anatomy of Performance

WHAT IS IT that separates a PGA Tour player from an amateur who plays once a week?

It sounds like a silly question with easy, obvious answers.

Talent.

Practice.

Single-minded dedication.

Access to first-class instruction.

All true, but secondary to the real point.

What if I told you that one of the main traits that separates tour players from you and me on the golf course—and world-beaters like Tiger Woods and Phil Mickelson from the "rank-and-file" players on the tour—has nothing to do with physical talent or beating thousands of balls on the range?

I've spent my career studying human performance, both in the lab and out in the world. My job is figuring out what makes people perform to the best of their abilities and clearing the roadblocks that stand in their way.

The real geniuses in sports—people like Michael Jordan in basketball, Serena Williams in tennis, Wayne Gretzky in hockey, and Tiger Woods in golf—unquestionably have incredible physical talent. But what really separates those giants from the rest is not their ability to manipulate a ball or their body in a certain way.

It's their ability to manipulate time.

You've probably heard athletes and announcers talk about how the game "slowed down" for them. Quarterbacks talk about the key moment when the scene from behind the offensive line wasn't total chaos but a chessboard, with the pieces moving in a choreographed dance. Baseball hitters talk about seeing pitches come in slow and fat—just waiting to be hit.

To those of us watching the action as spectators, time obviously doesn't actually slow down and wait for these players to do their thing.

It just seems like it does for them.

I know something about this from firsthand experience. I've played table tennis at a relatively high level for a number of years, and as a teenager I was ranked among the top handful of players in the United States. Still, there was a tier of players above me who were significantly better. At sixteen years old, I was playing one of them—six-time U.S. Open champion Dal-Joon Lee—when I found that place where the ball slows down, at least for a short time.

Watch a YouTube video of a match between two skilled table tennis players and you'll see that it's truly one of the fastest ball sports in the world. Players are hitting the ball in excess of 80 miles per hour across a table that is only nine feet long. It doesn't seem possible that the players can even react to what's happening.

But for the first hour of that match against Dal-Joon Lee, I was. I was connected to the ball. I could see it coming from every angle, and I was blocking and smashing it almost at will. I was ahead two sets and 13–7 in the third when a comment from one of my friends in the crowd—something to the effect that this would be the biggest upset in the sport at that time— broke the trance I was in, and I ended up losing.

For that short time, I had been in The Zone.

Table tennis was a challenging career path for a teenager in New York in those days, and after competing in the German professional league for a year and a half, I moved on to the premed program at Stanford. One of my earliest lab partners in organic chemistry was Eric Heiden, who had just finished winning all five of the individual speed skating gold medals at the 1980 Winter Olympics in Lake Placid. We became great friends, and it would fascinate me to hear him talk about his biggest races as if he had skated them in an empty rink, with nobody watching. Everything slowed down—even his pulse.

In one special class that Stanford convened for students with high-level athletic experience, Eric described how he was able to visualize every single stride he was about to make before his gold medal 5,000-meter race, and how he stumbled over a rut in the ice halfway through his 1,500-meter final but recovered in time to take another gold. Eric was the first person ever to win five individual gold medals in one Olympics—swimmer Michael Phelps matched him in 2008—and the very definition of this incredible mental acumen I've been describing.

As I made my way through my academic career at Stanford and the University of Texas and moved on to my internship in internal medicine at UCLA, my fascination with this kind of "timeless time" that great athletes would experience continued. It seemed that when a competitor was in the right state of consciousness, he or she could sample time in smaller and smaller increments. If you think of a fastball coming out of a pitcher's hand at 98 miles per hour, a hitter who is struggling might see that ball as a single frame. A photograph. But a locked-in Miguel Cabrera sees the ball as a movie—with thousands of frames. And when he's locked in like that, the movie slows down to the point where he can see the individual stitches on the ball, just as it slows down for a PGA Tour player when he can actually feel the position of the clubface at impact while the head is moving at 125 miles per hour.

I wanted to figure out what made the great ones like Eric—or Dal-Joon Lee—able to essentially live in The Zone, while other competitors could only visit it on occasion. Was it something inherently different in their makeup—like the physical difference between a six-foot-two point guard and a seven-foot-one center? Did their minds work differently?

And, most importantly, was it something an athlete could make happen more frequently through training?

The answer surprised me, and I'm sure it will surprise you too.

To figure it out, I engineered a study—which earned a grant from the United States Tennis Association—that measured the way different groups of athletes responded to light while under hypnosis. I based it on a technique developed by Dr. David Spiegel, a prominent psychiatrist at Stanford. Without getting too technical, Dr. Spiegel measured the changes in brain-processing speed on an EEG machine while people were under hypnosis—something extremely valuable in the study of disorders like Alzheimer's and Parkinson's diseases and ADD.

In my study, I used Dr. Spiegel's techniques on different groups of athletes, from world-class to competitive amateur triathletes to average "weekend warriors." I predicted that the study would show that those in the world-class group—which included my friend Eric Heiden, tennis player Roz Fairbanks, eight-time Ironman Triathlon champion Paula Newby-Fraser, Olympic miler Steve Scott, and gold-medal gymnast Peter Vidmar—would show that they received information more quickly than the average person and then processed it more quickly as well. In other words, their mental machine was in higher tune than those of us mortals.

But in reality my original prediction—that the signals would get there faster and stronger—didn't hold true. There *is* a correlation between being in top physical shape and processing information more quickly and efficiently. But the true world-class athletes didn't automatically process information any more quickly or efficiently than the group of fit amateur triathletes.

What they did do, however, was show the ability to consistently and consciously put themselves in a trancelike state that enhances performance. Simply put, the study seemed to indicate that peak athletic performance is more about state—the competitor's level of consciousness and ability to handle a given situation—than it is about trait, or some innate physical or mental wiring.

In other words, you can learn to find The Zone.

That's something with huge implications in the world of peak performance.

You've probably heard of *Outliers,* Malcolm Gladwell's runaway bestseller about the subject of human excellence. In it he advances Dr. K. Anders Ericsson's theory that a virtuoso in a given discipline—whether it's a sport, music, or surgery—has to devote ten thousand hours of directed practice to master the discipline.

We could argue about whether or not that's true, but I think the ten-thousand-hour theory misses the bigger point.

Don't get me wrong. Practice is certainly important. It's seductive to think that spending ten thousand hours—or five hours a day, five days a week, fifty weeks a year, for ten years—can overcome a real or perceived shortfall in actual physical talent. It might, to a degree, but there's no free ride. You do have to understand and improve the physical elements of any discipline to be good at it.

But it's *how* and *what* you practice that is fundamental to improvement. You have to practice intelligently, creatively—and over the entire spectrum of the body and mind. It's cliché, but your mind really *is* a muscle, and like all muscles it needs to be exercised to perform at its best.

Without understanding this fundamental concept, you will get only so far—literally and figuratively—with practice alone.

I've been affiliated with the U.S. Olympic Training Center outside San Diego for almost twenty years, and what's not missing over there is talent. The Olympic trials are filled with the most talented people you're ever going to find—in any discipline. They all have it, and they've all spent ten thousand hours practicing.

I even saw it with my brother.

In 1991, Brad qualified for the PGA Tour for the first time on his second try at qualifying school. I was in the middle of a research fellowship at the University of California, San Diego, and Brad asked me to come and caddie for him at the season-opening Sony Open in Hawaii. We worked together off and on for five years, including the 1993 PGA Tour Q-school finals, where John Feinstein immortalized Brad's ultimately successful quest in his famous book *A Good Walk Spoiled: Days and Nights on the PGA Tour.*

I not only saw how much work went into just surviving week to week on the tour, I also got to see how fine the line is between success and failure, and how little separates the "winners" from the "losers" in terms of physical skill.

Watching many of these incredibly talented athletes fail led to the big important question I wanted to answer in that research study, in my practice, and in this book:

In what ways can we train our minds to help us get the most out of our talent—whatever that talent happens to be?

Golf is democratic in that the average player goes through the same mental struggles a professional does. We all have our weaknesses and frailties, and the innate nature of all human minds is the same.

Through a rigorous process of trial and error over twenty years of work on the PGA Tour—which grew out of relationships that first developed during my time caddying for my brother—I came up with a system that helps players structure the mind's natural proclivities in a way that helps you play your best using innate logic, creativity, and instinct.

And it works just as well for players who want to win major championships as it does for ones who want to break 100 for the first time.

So much of mental training in golf is centered on general advice like "Stay in the moment" and "Focus on the process." It's not bad or inaccurate advice, as far as it goes. It's just incomplete. It's somewhat akin to learning how to drive a car, and the first pieces of advice you get as a beginner are to keep up with traffic and avoid crashing. Accurate but not useful.

You need a system to effectively integrate the new information.

It all starts with the Pre-Shot Pyramid—and the Six Components of Mental Excellence, which make up the blocks of the Pyramid.

1. Attitude
2. Motivation
3. Control
4. Optimization
5. Concentration
6. Planning

The first component, attitude, is just what it sounds like. It's your mind-set—and how you view yourself. Are you open to learning or blocked off? Are you a self-confident person? Are you assertive? Reticent? The elements of your attitude are the first indicator we investigate in the process.

Motivation gets at what drives you—from the primary level of fear and survival to the outer layers of material and emotional reward. The more you can understand your own personal motivations, the better

THE SIX COMPONENTS
OF MENTAL EXCELLENCE

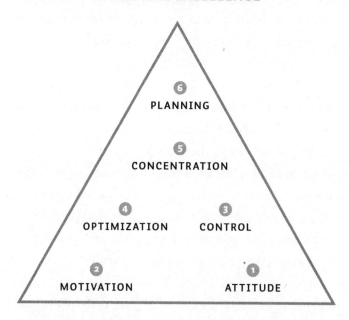

you can tailor your mental approach to take advantage of them.

Control has to do with how you're able to harness emotion. Many athletes have tremendous emotional control and play with a serene stoicism. Others burn hot, like John McEnroe, and thrive on that emotional turmoil. What's important to distinguish is the difference between productive tension and destructive anxiety—and what to do about both.

Optimization is where we start to move from the

"soft" discussion of thoughts and feelings to the literal work of applying skills and solutions in real-game situations. It's how to actually go about directing your thoughts and feelings to produce positive results.

Concentration, properly applied, is one of the main rewards for mastering these other skills. Productive players learn how and when to focus intensely and when to disconnect. To let the machine reset, so to speak.

To fully assemble the Pyramid, it is crucial to have an ultimate plan for what you want to accomplish and to understand the crucial distinction between skill acquisition and execution. The best players know how and when to train and how and when to compete. I'll show you how to do that in Chapter Seven.

Mastering Golf's Mental Game works in the same way my client sessions do. The goal is to assess how strong or weak you are in each of the components—for which the Mental Scorecard is perfectly designed. The information on each of the components (and the scorecard itself) found in the coming chapters will help you understand the components themselves and why you might be lacking in a particular area. You'll understand the theory behind the components and the "why" behind the way your mind works the way it does. The case studies and homework assignments will give you practical, real-world tools to incorporate the components into your game.

Why does it work?

Because the *Mastering Golf's Mental Game* system is designed to function in concert with the way we're already wired neurologically.

The biggest challenge I face when working with tour players is the fact that virtually every competitive player is inherently result-oriented.

Scores obviously matter.

But that strong results orientation often gets in the way of this trancelike focus we've been talking about, and prevents players from hitting each shot in the optimal mind-set. The Mental Scorecard system lets any player keep that natural results orientation but aim it at a better target, so to speak. You get to focus on results, but on results that actually make you play better, not worse!

Before we get started on the individual components of the Pyramid, I want to share a story about one of the first classes I took as an undergraduate at Stanford. I often tell my clients this story when they ask me how difficult it will be to improve. I like it because it neatly summarizes the frame of mind, openness, and focus you need to truly master something.

Before my friend Marty and I even walked into physics class our freshman year at Stanford, we were already intimidated. Both of us were still a little shell-shocked to even be in Palo Alto, surrounded by an academic crowd very different than the ones we were used to. Marty had transferred from Pomona College, where he was a linebacker on the football team, and I was a semiretired professional Ping-Pong player.

If we needed another reason to be scared, all we had to do was look at the professor. It was Dr. Arthur Schawlow, who just that year had won the Nobel Prize in physics for his pioneering work in laser spectroscopy.

Dr. Schawlow walked into the packed lecture hall and the buzz immediately went silent as he said, "Commence class."

Behind him on the stage hung a bowling ball suspended from a rope on the ceiling. Dr. Schawlow picked a student from the crowd to come and walk the ball to a raised platform to the side of the stage. As the student did this, Dr. Schawlow walked over to an identical platform on the opposite side of the stage.

Once they were in place, Dr. Schawlow told the student to release the ball.

We watched as it swung down on its rope, speeding up on a direct path toward the professor's head. It started to slow as it climbed on its arc, stopping about an inch from Dr. Schawlow's nose.

With a deadpan expression, he said, "Welcome to Physics 101."

We cheered, energized by the demonstration and

excited to learn what would come next. Of course, our mood changed a bit in the next few minutes when he went on to tell us what he expected.

"I don't give good grades unless you earn them," he said. "If you want to be a great runner, you run until it hurts. If you want to receive a good grade in my class, you learn physics until it hurts.

"This is your first and easiest class. Pick up your syllabus as you leave, and know Chapter One by Thursday.

"Class dismissed."

I tell you this for the same reason I tell it to my clients.

This system will help you get the most out of your game and the most out of your practice. But you'll still have to work at it.

It's time to roll up your sleeves and commence class.

CHAPTER 2

Attitude

A T ITS MOST basic level, the foundation of the Pre-Shot Pyramid starts in a place that should be familiar in a very visceral way.

We're talking about attitude, something you've undoubtedly heard about your entire life, whether it's been from a parent, a teacher, a spouse, or an employer. In simplest terms, attitude is your mental compass or alignment. It's your outlook on things and your self-confidence—or lack thereof.

The first step toward improving your mental approach in golf is to take inventory of your personal philosophies. That might sound a bit "soft" or high-brow, but I really mean it in a much more straightforward way. The first questions I ask a client have to do with where he or she stands on a few very broad and familiar scales.

Are you a competitive person? Are you more re-tiring and easygoing? Are you generally positive or pessimistic? Are you self-confident or are you self-conscious? As I listen to those answers, I'm comparing them to what I see for myself in front of me. Does the person's body language match what they're actually saying?

The reason we start with attitude is because it is a powerful trigger for all the things that come after. One of the most famous examples that prove this concept is the quest to run a mile in under four minutes.

For most of human history, the idea that a person could run a mile in less than four minutes was seen as outlandish fantasy. In the 1800s, amateur athletes were running a mile in about five minutes, and it wasn't until the 1940s that runners even began to approach what had previously seemed to be unattainable. Gun-der Hägg and Arne Andersson of Sweden traded the record back and forth throughout the 1940s, but no-body seemed to be able to crack the magic time.

By the 1950s, Roger Bannister was a relatively un-remarkable English track athlete who failed to earn a medal in the 1952 Olympics. Wavering over whether or not to quit the sport, he decided to dedicate himself to one great push to break the miraculous four-minute mark before he moved on to medical school. In 1954, at a meet at Oxford University, Bannister ran the mile in 3:59, finally breaking the four-minute mark and erasing Hägg's nine-year-old world record of 4:01.

Once Bannister showed the world that a sub-four-minute time was possible, other athletes approached their races with the attitude that they, too, could do it—not that it was something unattainable. Bannister's record-shattering time only lasted forty-six days before Australian John Landy registered a time of 3:58. By the 1970s, runners were routinely recording times below 3:50, and the current record is 3:43, by Hicham El Guerrouj of Morocco.

The golfer's mind works in the same ways. My brother came up through the ranks with Rich Beem, who would go on to win the Kemper Open as a rookie on the PGA Tour in 1999—and, most famously, the 2002 PGA Championship. Rich, my brother, and I were hanging out one night early in a tournament week when Rich told my brother he had what it took to win on tour. "If I did, you can too," he said. "It's like walking through a door."

As simple as that sounds, Rich was right. The players who break through and win a major for the first time—or a first PGA Tour event, or even just break a scoring goal at the amateur level—aren't any different physically than they were the week before they won. They just transitioned to seeing the task as an opportunity, not something daunting or scary.

I don't like to make sweeping statements when it comes to neuroscience, but one of the most fascinating things about this business is the fact that the mental barriers and "issues" of the golfers I meet as clients transcend the players' level of achievement. Sure, the guy who is trying to break into the top twenty in the world has some different details to discuss than the person trying to break 100 for the first time. But the fundamental anxieties and struggles we have as players are universal.

They're human.

Whether you're a tour player or a 20-handicapper, you have what can be called a personal "style"—both in terms of how you think and how you swing. One of the most common crises I see is when a player gets lost or separated from his or her personal style. In simple terms, you're a lot less effective when you're trying to impersonate somebody else.

Case Study

Eddie had a very solid career as a tour player for many years, but he never felt like he reached his true potential. He was a multiple-season All-America as a college player and had beaten soundly many of the players who would go on to become top twenty professionals.

In his third year on tour, Eddie played against one of the top two or three players in the world head-to-head down the stretch and made a big mistake on the last hole, to lose the tournament by a shot.

He won an event in the next couple of years, but he couldn't shake the nagging feeling that he wasn't as fundamentally sound as the top players in the world—and that he wouldn't get to that level unless he made some big changes.

That began a process where he bounced from swing instructor to swing instructor. One season he worked with three different coaches over a six-month span. The third of those coaches actually referred Eddie to me, because he saw that the issues weren't so much swing related as they were confidence related.

By this time Eddie had gotten so far away from what he used to do in his quest for the "perfect" swing that he couldn't remember how to make his own swing—the one that had earned him a full-ride scholarship and more than $10 million in prize money. He was going from tournament to tournament trying to make the latest swing he had learned work, and had become nothing more than a fringe tour player.

Eddie came out to San Diego for a few days and we talked in-depth about the times in his career when he felt the most comfortable. He said that at the end of his college career and his first year as a professional he'd played with almost a kind of tunnel vision naiveté. We watched some video of his swing from that time, and it actually wasn't much different from what he was doing now. I suggested Eddie get back with the coach he had at the beginning of his career and make simplifying and relaxing his two main goals for the next three months.

Eddie's first coach had a long track record with him and knew how to handle what they were going to do. He assured Eddie that he was very close, and a small, individual change in one of his fundamentals would put him not just where he needed to be but where he used to be.

We also spent some time talking about the concept of redefining "winning." Tournament victories are obviously a goal, but I wanted Eddie to see that the ultimate competition wasn't against the guys he used to beat in college. His game was good enough to stand on its own, and the only yardstick to compare himself to was how prepared he was physically and mentally. The results would speak for themselves.

A few months later Eddie was six shots off the lead going into the final round. He came out and birdied four of the first six holes to take the lead, then ran away with the tournament on the back nine.

I talked to him that night to see how he was processing what had happened, and he was obviously excited. The first thing he said was that he didn't feel like he did anything out of the ordinary. He just hit a bunch of shots he knew he could hit.

PERFECT SWING

One of the harder lessons to learn in modern tour golf is that there are no trophies or checks for "perfect swings." Unless a player owns the swing he or she has and is able to make the necessary adjustments when out there alone in the heat of the battle, all the theories and philosophies any coach can give don't have much value.

One of the most memorable moments of my caddying career came at the Sony Open in Hawaii in 1994, the first event of the season. I was standing behind my brother, cleaning his clubs as he warmed up next to a rookie who had his father caddying for him.

It was Jim Furyk.

Jim and my brother were good friends, and I could understand why. Jim was a no-nonsense, blue-collar kind of guy and a high school jock, just like my brother was.

But Jim had one of the truly funky swings on the PGA Tour. It didn't look anything like those postcard-perfect ones you see Adam Scott or Justin Rose make. We split up to go play, and Jim wound up scraping it around at about par for two days and missing the cut.

Watching Jim warm up that day, I actually felt bad for him, because I didn't think he had a chance to have any kind of professional career. I mentioned this to my brother later, and he quickly corrected me. Brad said Jim was the real deal and that nobody he knew had more trust in his swing. In the world of tour golf, there's almost no better compliment you can give.

That week my brother beat Jim by six shots—and $3,300—but Jim has gone on to become the fourth leading money winner of all time and the 2003 U.S. Open champion. All with a swing and a putting stroke that are the definition of "homemade."

Just think about how tough and resilient Jim has had to be over the years. He's no doubt heard all of the cracks about his swing looking like an octopus in a phone booth. During down periods, a weaker player would have considered making changes to become more "orthodox." Jim famously snap-hooked his tee shot on the 16th hole to throw away a chance to win his second U.S. Open, in 2012 at the Olympic Club in San Francisco. And he missed putts on the 17th and 18th holes that would have won a crucial match in the Ryder Cup later that same year. But there he was at the PGA Championship in 2013, taking on Jason Dufner down the stretch at forty-three years old. He's never hit the ball the longest or had the most talent, but he perseveres, and he plays his own game.

That's the quality you want to copy as a player—not some impossibly fit twenty-five-year-old's swing.

THE CUT LINE

The PGA Tour is pretty ruthless. If you don't perform, you won't be around long. Players get lumped into one of two categories pretty quickly upon arrival. You're either a guy who isn't afraid to put himself on the line—win or lose—or you're a rabbit who's just trying to make cuts and stay out there.

The distinction between the two groups has softened a bit over time because there's so much more money to be made even as you move down the earnings list. Back in the day, the check for finishing second wasn't going to change Jack Nicklaus's life. He wanted the trophy. But a $10,000 check for second place at the Masters in the 1960s could make a player's year—and mean the difference between staying out on tour the next season and going home and finding a job selling insurance.

Today there's a good living to be made even at seventy-five or one hundred on the money list in the men's game. And there are players out there who have as their focus making cuts first and then recording top twenty-fives.

I don't point these players out to criticize their talent level. You have to be an incredible player to even get to the PGA Tour once.

I make the point because the players who are talented enough to get to the PGA Tour are talented enough to win there, but their attitude and expectation get in the way!

My brother would be the first to tell you that that happened to him. He played five years on the PGA Tour, but I don't think he ever felt truly comfortable or like he really belonged. He's a shy guy, and I think he spent so much mental energy just going through the Q-school process to make it time after time that he was, in a way, used up by the time the season came. He made a lot of cuts, but unless you're contending and getting chances to win, you don't stay out there long-term.

For a long time Ken Duke was a journeyman pro who didn't hit it great but hung on thanks to a terrific short game. He bounced around from the Canadian Tour to the Web.com Tour and flunked out a couple of times on the PGA Tour. But the light went on in 2013, and he won his first PGA Tour event—at age forty-four—by hitting it to three feet for birdie on the 2nd hole of a playoff at the Travelers Championship in Connecticut.

There was a switch, and it stopped being about made cuts and started being about winning tournaments.

Justin Rose figured out how to pull the same switch—not just once but twice. When he turned pro, Rose famously missed the first twenty-one cuts of his career. After finishing fourth at European Tour Q-school, he struggled so badly the next season he lost his card again. But by 2003 he was consistently in the top fifty in the world rankings—even though he had notable trouble playing with the lead in majors. It obviously wasn't about making cuts for him anymore— and he proved it at the 2013 U.S. Open. He played wonderful golf down the stretch to win his first major by a shot over Phil Mickelson. Two of the other major winners that year, Adam Scott and Jason Dufner, also took similar extended paths to their first big win. Scott had been anointed as the next Tiger Woods when he turned pro in 2000 but hadn't lived up to that billing in the majors before winning the Masters in dramatic style over Angel Cabrera. Despite elite ball-striking skills, Dufner labored for seven years in the minor leagues before breaking through with two wins on the PGA Tour in 2012. He followed that with the PGA win over Furyk.

If you aren't playing professional golf—or even competitive golf—what does this mean to you? It works the same way. Your attitude and expectations set the parameters for how you will play, no matter what the stakes are.

There is always a mental cut line.

When you become obsessed with a certain scoring target—whether it's the number you need to make a cut or the golf equivalent of Roger Bannister's 3:59 mile—you run the risk of creating mental barriers for yourself that distract you from the job at hand. At the amateur level, I see it all the time with players who dream of breaking 80 for the first time—or 100, or 70.

The secret to scaling these self-imposed mental barriers is to change the way you set goals and think about reaching them. I love the programs golf instructors Lynn Marriott and Pia Nilsson have developed out in Arizona. They're called Vision54 and are based on the idea that you can go out and make eighteen birdies.

The most successful players do a better job both setting goals and thinking about their progress toward those goals. One of the key factors in becoming one of these players is adjusting and improving something called *mind-set*.

MIND-SET

Listen closely to the way different players talk to the media after a loss and you can hear two very distinct, opposite viewpoints.

Take tennis star Rafael Nadal, who had just lost to Novak Djokovic in the finals of the 2011 U.S. Open—Nadal's sixth straight loss to Djokovic. "You know, I like the fight. I want to enjoy the battle against him," Nadal said. "Six straight losses—for sure that's painful, but I'm going to work every day until that changes. So I have a goal. To have a goal, always you know how to work every day."

Compare that statement to the one Sergio García made throwing off any responsibility for a particularly painful loss to Pádraig Harrington at the 2007 British Open. His tee shot on the par-3 16th in the playoff hit the pin and bounced off the green, leading to a bogey. "It's not the first time, unfortunately. I don't know . . . I'm playing against a lot of guys out there. More than just the field," Garcia said. "To tell you the truth, I really didn't feel like I did anything wrong. I really didn't miss a shot out there in the playoff. I hit unbelievable putts. They just didn't go in."

Stanford professor Dr. Carol Dwek wrote a popular book called *Mindset: The New Psychology of Success,* which lays out the two general viewpoints from which people see their performance: a growth mind-set and a fixed mind-set.

A player with what Dwek calls a growth mind-set believes success is based on hard work, training, and openness to learning new skills. On the other side of the spectrum, a player with what Dwek calls a fixed mind-set believes his or her success is based on innate ability, and they fear failure because it hurts their perception of themselves.

MIND-SET CONTINUUM

FIXED   GROWTH

It isn't hard to peg Nadal with the growth mind-set and Garcia with the fixed mind-set. And it isn't a surprise to see that Nadal would go on to beat Djokovic in the French Open final the next spring—and that he was able to adapt his dominant clay-court style to win two Wimbledon titles on grass. Meanwhile, García would continue to struggle in major championships— even going as far to say at the 2012 Masters that he didn't think he would even win one. "I don't have the capacity to win a major," he said. "It's the reality. I'm not good enough, and I know it."

It should come as no surprise that Dwek's research shows that people who approach things with a growth mind-set live less stressful, more successful lives. The good news is that even if you're more inclined toward the fixed side of the scale, you can shift the balance to the better with a little work.

Your first challenge is to assess your own mind-set and determine if you need to make some changes.

Homework

Based on what you've just learned about mind-set, ask yourself some simple performance-related questions about your golf game.

- Am I a good player?
- Have I improved over the last five years?
- Can I win my club championship (or other event that matters to you)?

- Can I hit all of the shots I want to hit, when I want to hit them?
- Most times, do I feel satisfied after I've played?

Think about your answers, then make sure you ask yourself at least five questions like the examples I've just given, and, with a pencil, mark where on the continuum curve (below) you think you are and date it.

MIND-SET CONTINUUM

Avoided	**CHALLENGES**	Embraced
Ignored	**CRITICISMS**	Learned from
Threatened	**OTHERS' SUCCESS**	Inspired

FIXED   **GROWTH**

Go through the same process after you've finished reading this book. Then do it again every three months for the next year. If you find that you innately have a growth mind-set, you can move on to another area of focus. Most players fall on the fixed side of the mind-set spectrum.

If you find yourself in the strong fixed-mind-set category, don't despair. The exercises in this and other chapters will help you move to a more balanced position. And plenty of players have been in the same boat as you and made dramatic improvements.

Two great examples are Steve Stricker and Phil Mickelson.

When Steve originally came onto the PGA Tour in 1994, he was very good, but he was very tense and hard on himself. He saw a lot of success early on, winning two tournaments in 1996 and finishing fourth on the money list. In 2001 he won the WCG Match Play—and the $1 million check that went with it. But by 2004, a bad slump and a variety of injuries basically sent Steve back home to Madison, Wisconsin. It took him two years to regain his swing and his confidence, and he came back to the tour a different guy. He was healthier, happier, more relaxed, and more open. He did a much better job processing his negative feelings and letting them go. The next thing you know, he's making history well into his forties. He's won nine times since 2007, including three straight times at his hometown John Deere Classic.

Phil Mickelson is definitely not a fixed-mind-set guy in general, but he always approached the British Open in a fixed way. He believed that his kind of high-ball, high-spin kind of game wasn't suited for links golf, and that the British would always be the hardest major for him to win. But in 2013 he came in with a much more open mind-set. He accepted that the course wasn't going to be perfect for him, but he believed he was talented enough to find the right shots and could play well enough to win. He wasn't going to write it off. Sure enough, he played some of the best golf of his life and won at Muirfield last summer.

One of the joys of golf for both the tour guys and regular handicap players is that life doesn't end at forty. This isn't football or track. You can continue to improve and hit the ball better as you get older. The players who get passed by are the ones who start telling themselves they're too old or that the younger guys hit it too far. They stay in place. They stop going to the gym and they give up and "accept" their lot in life—a fixed mind-set.

Keep your foot on the accelerator and keep playing to win and embracing that challenge, and you'll love the game even when you don't get the results you hoped for.

RESULTS VERSUS PROCESS ORIENTATION

One of the big advantages of using the Mental Scorecard we're going to talk about in the second part of this book is that it gives you a way to be results oriented in a way that improves your process.

I want to take a minute to explain what that means and why it's important.

Imagine you're in school and you have a big exam coming up. It's crucial for you to do well.

How do you approach it?

If you're a results-oriented person, you're hyper-focused on getting a good grade. You're obsessed with the score itself, which can certainly cause anxiety, which is counterproductive to performing well.

If you're hyperfocused on your preparation for the test—acquiring the knowledge you're going to need and figuring out what you'll need to do to stay cool and think clearly—you're operating in a process-oriented way.

When you're process oriented, you're able to immerse yourself in what you're doing at the moment, without being distracted by the eventual outcome or score. In results-oriented mode, you're constantly evaluating your performance, both subjectively and in terms of score.

There are times when being results oriented is good—like on the practice range. That's where you're working on things like gaining distance or hitting clubs specific distances. But for the most part, being process oriented is the ideal we're trying to get to in golf.

It's not as easy as flipping a switch, but you can certainly adjust your orientation. All of the homework exercises in this book are going to help you move from being results oriented toward being process oriented. As with the fixed-versus-growth scale, it's important to figure out where you fall in the process-versus-results spectrum so you can measure your progress as you make your way through this book.

Homework

Take a moment to think about your immediate and long-term goals with your golf game. Are they results or process oriented?

Results Orientation
- Scoring goal (break 90, 80)
- Distance goal (hit driver 20 more yards)
- Statistical goal (hit more fairways, greens)

Process Orientation
- Complete routine before hitting any shot
- Improve visualization
- Compile accurate club distances

Figure an overall score for your orientation and place a mark representing it on the process versus results continuum curve on page 46. Date it and come back and reevaluate your position when you've finished this book.

PROCESS-VERSUS-RESULTS ASSESSMENT TOOL

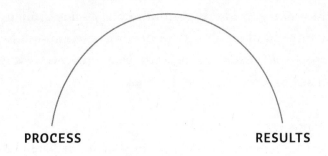

PROCESS   **RESULTS**

SELF-CONFIDENCE

The factors we've been discussing mix together in a unique brew called self-confidence. What we're really trying to do here is build self-confidence and create a reliable process to use before every shot you hit.

The term "self-confidence" itself has become a kind of pop psychology catchall term for feeling good about yourself, but I want to use it in a more specific way here. Self-confidence is really self-efficacy—the belief that you can accomplish your goals. And there is a definite science and art to self-efficacy.

The definitive model for defining self-efficacy was built by Dr. Albert Bandura some forty years ago, and it still works very well. In simplified form, it breaks down into three core components: vicarious learning, social persuasion, and mastery experiences.

Pulling it out of science-speak, think of confidence as a three-layer cake with three separate, distinct ingredients. The first, vicarious learning, is the ability to model yourself after somebody and learn so you can do what he or she does. The second, social persuasion, is getting support and reinforcement from friends, family, and associates. The third, mastery experiences, is actually accomplishing a step toward your goal and validating for yourself that you're ready for the next step.

The path to improving self-confidence is fairly straightforward: Study the success of others. Benefit from being around positive-minded people who encourage you to have your own successes and persevere through failures. And finally, as you begin to have successes, remind yourself of those successes to reinforce your positive feelings about yourself.

I've had the privilege of working with PGA Tour player Rich Beem for more than ten years, and his is the perfect story of building self-confidence. In 1994, Rich got out of New Mexico State and decided to give pro golf a try. He didn't have much success and quit the game to enter the business world. He was selling cell phones in Seattle when he saw that a college friend, J. P. Hayes, had won on the PGA Tour. Rich saw what J.P. had done to get to that level and decided it was something he could model for his own game. With the encouragement of his friends and coaches, he worked on his game and went back to Q-school in 1998. He earned a card that year and won the Kemper Open as a rookie in 1999. Three years later, in 2002, Rich got hot and won his second PGA Tour event (another mastery experience), the International at Castle Rock, Colorado. Later that month, brimming with confidence, Rich won the PGA Championship.

Within the context of your own game and life, you can build your own set of reference points and targets. Maybe your model is a player at your club who took up golf in his thirties, worked hard with the pro, and got down to a 10 handicap over the course of two years. Your peer group could be the pro at your club, a trusted playing partner, a spouse, or a sport psychologist. And your mastery experience could be winning the B flight of your club championship, taking all three ways of a $10 Nassau from your nemesis, or qualifying for the city amateur tournament.

Use the next homework assignment to put those pieces in place.

Homework
Read the boxes in the middle and left side of the diagram on page 49. Write your responses in the empty

boxes on the right. I want you to revisit this exercise intermittently: It will build your confidence and help you play better.

CONFIDENCE HOMEWORK

LAYERS	DETAILS & DIRECTIONS	YOU FILL OUT
Vicarious Learning (modeling others' behaviors)	List players you want to emulate and why	
Social Persuasion	Talk with a sport psychologist or friends that act like one!	
Mastery Experiences	List and describe your best rounds	

Now that we've covered the basics of attitude and you've completed some homework assignments, you're ready to take your first exam. Pass it, and you'll be fully armed with the knowledge you need to take control of your attitude both on and off the course.

EXAM

The following six statements are actual quotes from PGA Tour players. Some of them are examples of process-related thinking, some pertain to mind-set, and some are examples of both. Read them and check the appropriate box.

STATEMENT 1

I don't like to play a course where the tee shots are all tight, and I always play poorly at U.S. Opens.

Mind-set

☐ Fixed   ☐ Growth

STATEMENT 2

The younger players just hit the ball farther and farther, and I can't keep up with them.

Mind-set

☐ Fixed   ☐ Growth

STATEMENT 3

When the play is this slow, I love it because I know half the players are so annoyed, they'll play badly and I won't.

Mind-set

☐ Fixed   ☐ Growth

STATEMENT 4

I always start out terribly; just once I need to birdie the 1st hole.

Attitude

☐ Process ☐ Result

STATEMENT 5

It's been so long, I'd really like to win this week. But I don't want to get ahead of myself. I know what I have to do: stay patient, be committed to each shot, and make good decisions.

Attitude

☐ Process ☐ Result

STATEMENT 6

Every time I'm about to go low and shoot 63 or 64, I choke and give it away on 17 or 18.

Mind-set **Attitude**

☐ Fixed ☐ Growth ☐ Process ☐ Result

IN STATEMENT 1

The comment "I always play poorly at U.S. Opens" clearly shows a fixed mind-set. A growth mind-set alternative is: "Although I don't have the best track record at U.S. Opens, I've been working hard on my game—keeping my drives in play and hitting 3-wood on very tight holes. I'm looking forward to embracing the challenge."

IN STATEMENT 2

Again we have a fixed mind-set that sets the player up for failure. Better to be productive and say, "They don't give the winner a trophy for driving distance but for score—and regardless of what the big hitters are doing, the scoring average that wins the Vardon Trophy hasn't changed much in thirty years. Instead of being intimidated, I'll use my experience to my advantage."

IN STATEMENT 3

This is obviously a growth-mind-set comment. The player embraces the condition of slow play as a challenge rather than an obstacle.

IN STATEMENT 4

We have a results-oriented statement evidenced by the need to birdie the 1st hole. What happens if, while the ball is in the air, there's a huge gust of wind that blows a good drive a few feet off line into an impossible lie in the rough? If your thinking is completely results oriented—that is, making a birdie on this hole—then you're already on your way to a losing game. Instead, say: "Today I'm spending a little more time warming up. I'll see if I can't get a competitive game going around the practice green before tee time. That might allow me to have a better start."

IN STATEMENT 5

The player sounds like he or she is starting to put un-needed pressure on him- or herself to win, but recovers by making process-oriented goals that focus on patience, execution, and good decision making.

IN STATEMENT 6

The player makes two errors here: endorsing both a fixed ("I can't go low") and a results-oriented mind-set (focusing on the score of 63 or 64). A process orientation would focus on each shot, not the score. Also, why not be inventive? Imagine playing twenty-one holes, so when you come down to 16, 17, and 18, you won't feel all the pressure you usually feel when you're doing well with three holes to go.

CHAPTER 3

Motivation

L IFE IS ABOUT motivation.

It's the why that drives you to do the things you do—and to avoid the things you avoid—every day.

It's the reason we work and play, and it influences every relationship we have.

In the big picture, you could be motivated by love, money, power, or fame. In day-to-day life, your personal motivation strongly determines how you perform at your job and how well you perform in a sport like golf.

What motivates *you* in particular might seem like the most personal thing in the world—and it is—but it fits into one of three broad categories that apply to all of us. Cracking the textbook for a minute, we see that basic motivational theory divides motivators into three segments with not terribly creative names: primary, secondary, and tertiary. Labeling these categories in this way—essentially first, second, and third—has to do with where they fit in the biological imperative. In simple terms, they're ordered based on how important they are to ensuring survival.

Why is it important to distinguish between the different kinds of motivation? Because the different flavors of motivation are best handled in different ways, and they all work with a different degree of efficiency. I like to describe motivation as the fuel that makes your engine work. Low-octane gas can get the job done, but the engine probably works better on high-quality, high-octane fuel.

Let's take a quick tour through the three kinds of motivation. See if you can recognize some of what drives you within them.

PRIMARY MOTIVATION

Fear is the granddaddy of all motivators. It's hardwired into our brains in the form of survival instinct. Your mind and body have been conditioned through thousands of years of evolution to make snap judgments about your environment. Am I safe? Is something important to me being threatened? Fight or flight? You can think of primary motivators as the basic human responses—hunger, thirst, pain avoidance, sex drive, fear, aggression. They're the instincts that kept our prehistoric ancestors alive in a landscape filled with danger.

Golf is something most of us do for fun, but primary motivation can certainly come into play for a professional when their livelihood is on the line. Lee Trevino left school at fourteen to work as a caddie, and his golf skills provided him with a way to support his extended family from a young age. He joined the tour relatively late at age twenty-eight after building his bankroll in head-to-head money games with hustlers around Dallas. When asked about the pressure of PGA Tour golf, he joked that real pressure was playing for $5 a hole when you had no money in your pocket. Winning a match was literally the difference between eating and not eating.

You would think that modern tour players playing for millions in prize money wouldn't face such stark challenges, but I can tell you that the fear of losing playing privileges in mid-career—and shutting off that strong income stream on which a large lifestyle has been built—can have a paralyzing effect. I've seen it destroy careers, or at least seriously derail them for years at a time.

SECONDARY MOTIVATION

Once you get beyond the basic human drives, you get to secondary, or learned, motivations. An easy way to peg secondary motivations is to think about the way parents reward and punish behavior in children. Based on his or her parents' actions, a child learns what kinds of behavior are acceptable or unacceptable. Pick up your plate and take it to the sink after a meal and receive praise and a cookie. Write on the wall with a marker and go to the corner for a time-out. Miss your curfew and you can't go out Friday night and you're not allowed to use the car.

Most of civilized life is built upon secondary motivations you (hopefully) learned as a child. When you go to school, studying and performing well on tests results in good grades. Good grades can get you into a good school—and eventually into a good job—so you're motivated to do the necessary work. You're delaying the instant gratification that would come with sleeping in, playing video games, or staying out late with friends in exchange for the long-term benefits of a good degree and job that come from staying in and studying for that test. It works the same way in the professional world: If you work hard, you can put yourself in line for a bonus and a promotion.

At both the amateur and professional levels, secondary motivation rules most of the action. When you're playing a $5 Nassau with a friend, your play is motivated by the desire for bragging rights—and the desire not to have to reach into your wallet at the end of the afternoon. At the tour level, players have to balance maintaining a schedule that keeps them fresh and connected with their families with the draw of making more money by playing more events or doing more sponsor outings.

TERTIARY MOTIVATION

For years, scientists believed that the first two levels of motivation accounted for the complete human condition. But, as is usually the case, things aren't as simple as they seem.

About fifty years ago, Dr. Harry Harlow performed a groundbreaking series of experiments on motivation using monkeys in his primate lab in Madison, Wisconsin. He set up a labyrinth filled with tasks for his monkeys and operated on the basic assumption that a series of food treats would enhance their motivation toward completing the tasks and improve their performance.

But before the study even began, he noticed something fascinating.

The monkeys began performing the tasks without any prompting, and without any rewards.

Instead of starting his planned experiment, Dr. Harlow began documenting what the monkeys were doing on their own. They continued to be motivated to complete the tasks without any intervention from the scientists.

At that point Dr. Harlow supposed that adding in punishments and rewards for the monkeys' performance on the tasks would increase their productivity beyond what they were accomplishing on their own. But the opposite happened.

Once the monkeys were rewarded and punished for their productivity, both their motivation and productivity decreased. This simple observation opened a whole new discussion in motivation theory.

The result?

Now we know that having the opportunity to be creative and autonomous increases motivation. In fact, it produces what I consider to be the "purest" kind of motivation: passion.

When you love what you're doing—whether it's a job or a hobby—you don't need anybody to make you get up in the morning to go do it. You don't struggle to find the time in the day to make it happen.

Tertiary motivation is the premium gas that often

produces the highest level of performance from any player, whether a pro or an amateur.

Ironically, it's usually the tour player who has the most trouble maintaining tertiary motivation for the game, even with all the "benefits" that come with being a professional athlete. At the highest levels, players earn millions of dollars, and they have fans, sponsors, and media clamoring for their time. Once the money and fame become the driving forces for continuing to play the sport, these *external motivations* replace the *internal motivation* that is love or passion for the game itself—the joy of doing what you do.

It should come as no surprise that when you're doing anything for the pure joy of it—whether it's golf or any other pastime—you're going to be less self-conscious about it and more excited to do it, and you're generally going to perform better. When a tour player gets to be too focused on rankings, earnings, and income, they can add pressure above and beyond the natural pressure that comes with playing at the highest level.

Case Study

In 2001, sixteen-year-old phenom Ty Tryon turned professional and made the cut at the Honda Classic on the PGA Tour—an incredible achievement. The next year he made it through the grueling qualifying school and earned a fully-exempt tour card as a seventeen-year-old high school senior—again, a once-in-a-generation achievement.

Before long, Ty had signed multiple lucrative contracts with Red Bull, Nike, and a host of other sponsors. Those sponsors obviously wanted to get their money's worth out of their new star, and they expected Ty—in addition to playing on tour—to keep a demanding schedule of corporate appearances and events with clients.

It's important to note that these kinds of responsibilities are "par for the course" on the PGA Tour—and part of life as a sponsored athlete. Sponsors pay the bills in a very real way, both by backing tournaments and by offering sponsorship money that can cushion a player in a sport like golf, which has little or no guaranteed prize money.

But asking a seventeen-year-old to learn how to budget his time and attention that way is different from expecting a thirty-five-year-old to do it after working up to that level of responsibility over ten or fifteen years.

Early in his pro career, Ty visited with me in San Diego and told me his life traveling on tour was difficult and he wished he could be doing more fun things and spending more time with friends back home.

It all made obvious sense. The PGA Tour is a business, and although everyone for the most part is very nice, players are competing fiercely for survival. It's not necessarily the healthiest place for a high school senior. On tour you get up really early to play through all kinds of weather, and you have to train and practice even if you don't feel like it. Playing on tour is a job, and it's easy to lose your passion when you forget to play for fun. At that time Ty lost some of his *internal motivation* because his *external motivation*—sponsor responsibility and the push to earn money—became overwhelming.

Ty lost his card after that first season and has spent the last ten years on various tours, trying to work his way back to the PGA Tour—this time as a seasoned mini-tour player instead of a phenom.

THE BEST WAY to help any player find the best motivational fuel in golf is to reconnect them with their passion for the sport. Internal, tertiary motivation always trumps external, secondary motivation.

What's interesting about Phil Mickelson is that it isn't about money. It isn't about fame. He loves golf, and we have a lot of conversations about why that is. He is extremely creative in his play, and it probably isn't a surprise that his practice follows the same pattern. This creativity and willingness to learn and try new shots is a big part of the passion and fun he has for the game. And it's that passion that drives his hard work, which in turn allows him to play at the highest level on the PGA Tour. He is motivated by his love for golf, and this is why after winning more than forty tour events and five major championships he stays hungry.

Another important piece of the puzzle for Phil is that he has perspective about the place the game holds in his life. Golf is obviously an important thing, and it has provided an incredible life for him and his family. But it's still just one thing, and it isn't who he is. Being a golfer is what he does. Arnold Palmer said his father taught him that golf was a game and to treat it—and the people you meet around it—as such. Palmer had fun when he played, and he had passion like Phil does. It's probably not a coincidence that they have similar playing styles and wear their joy on their sleeves.

We love games, and passion makes us free.

Homework

Ask yourself: "Why do I play golf?" Do you wish you'd practice harder and make the game more of a priority? Do you play to have fun or impress your friends? Now take a moment and check the box in the following motivation test that best fits your assessment of your own motivation.

MOTIVATION TEST

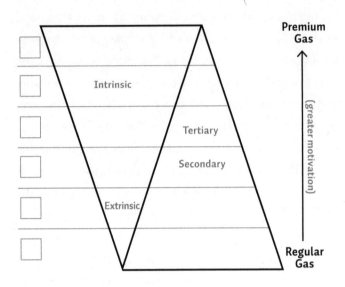

It should be clear by now that tertiary motivation is the premium one we're all searching for. But the problem for all of us—whether you're a professional golfer, a doctor, or a person in any other line of work—is that even when you have a lot of it, it can flag or burn out. Life is hectic, and it can burn anyone out from time to time.

Using the tour player example again, some clients come to me and say they're struggling with their drive to continue working at the level that got them to where they are. It often happens when a player starts a family, and it gets harder and harder to go on the road for weeks at a time when you have a new life with little kids at home.

For them, golf becomes a tedious job—one that they endure instead of enjoy.

At first you might think that there aren't any parallels between that experience and the one you might have as a recreational player. But there's no question that many people proclaim how much they love the sport but grind themselves up with anger and self-loathing when they actually participate in it. And, worse yet, they're doing that to themselves voluntarily—as a hobby.

The standard advice you always hear in those burnout scenarios is to put the clubs away and take a break. Sometimes just realizing that you don't have to be great all the time—and that freshness is important—can take some of the pressure off. One of the big advantages of the increasing purses on the PGA Tour over the last ten years is the financial freedom it gives many players to take more control over their schedules. But at other times a vacation doesn't address the underlying problem.

If you're suffering from that lack of motivation, you need to try to put yourself in position to fall in love with the game again. I know it sounds like corny marriage-therapy advice, but it really is true. I've worked with players who had a complete renaissance in their outlook simply by thinking back to the times they played the game with their fathers on summer afternoons. I've taken them back to the times in high school or college when they got up and went out to play nine holes alone just after dawn—for the love of the sport. One woman found the fire again by going back to her hometown and spending a week playing nine-hole rounds with her old high school teammates, riding in the cart, and laughing.

It's in there. It just needs to be accessed. The dots need to be connected.

As counterintuitive as it may sound, fear—the granddaddy motivator of them all—can also be a productive way to reconnect with that missing drive.

Used properly, fear is terrific gasoline. It makes you hyperalert and ready for action. I'm sure you can think of several instances in your life when the thought of angering or disappointing a parent, boss, teacher, or other authority figure gave you a jolt of fear. Fear of failure certainly fueled my determination to pass my national medical boards.

Some of my clients thrive on fear, and it is something we use in our talks. Nate Kaeding carved a ten-year career in the NFL as a kicker by using fear to drive his workouts. Rich Beem made the PGA Tour and became a major championship winner because he spent hours at the range out of fear that other competitors were going to pass him by.

Fear certainly has its negative aspects, but it's a normal part of being human. We all feel it to a lesser or greater extent, depending on how we're strung. It is part of the emotional experience—and emotions are what give us energy. The goal here is to take that energy and direct in a positive way, which we're going to talk more about in Chapter Four.

Pulling back from the world of professional golf, let's talk about the recreational player. Lack of motivation can be the crisis that drives you from the game for good. Or it can be a more subtle problem that keeps you from reaching your potential. For example, you enjoy getting out and playing with your friends, but you don't bother with practicing.

"Why" questions are the operative tool here. If you don't have any interest in practice, ask yourself why. Are you legitimately short on time? That could be, but in my experience, even the busiest executives and CEOs find the time to hit balls if they're interested in playing better.

A more likely scenario is that you're worried, consciously or subconsciously, that even if you practice, you won't improve. By avoiding practice, you give yourself an easy out when you talk about your game. "I shot 92 today, but it's no surprise—I never get a chance to practice." It's no different than when a professional essentially sabotages him- or herself by not practicing because he or she isn't ready or doesn't want the attention and pressure that comes with getting into contention. It's much more common than you think.

Recreational players can also suffer a kind of burnout. It's different than what a tour player goes through after ten years of thirty events per season, but I see plenty of amateurs in their forties and fifties who simply get tired of hitting the same kinds of bad shots. It can even be something as simple as not wanting to deal with the five and a half hours that a round at a public course can easily take.

Of course, the stakes for you and me quitting the game aren't the same as they are for a tour player who is supporting him- or herself and a family. Still, some of the other techniques for reconnecting work the same for a professional as they do for an amateur.

Perspective is a big part of the answer. With a tour player, I might lightheartedly suggest that he or she go take a shift or two at Starbucks making $10 an hour and compare that to the earning potential as a professional golfer. Perspective is also having the ability to see that the game is made up of many different parts and that disliking one or two of the parts doesn't mean you pitch out the whole.

You might struggle mightily off the tee, and those

struggles run the risk of corroding your enjoyment of the game overall. But perspective hopefully lets you see the other, better parts of the game: time with friends, being outside, making a long putt. It's the same process I use to help tour players keep the parts of the job they don't like—dealing with the media, or getting on a plane every week—separate from the parts they love. Once you can put those things in context—understanding that they're parts of the job that make it possible to live this lifestyle—it becomes easier to let go of the frustration surrounding them.

Another way to address a motivational "clog" is to change the way you play the game. So much of golf gets tied up in scores and handicaps that sometimes it's a great break to mix things up and challenge yourself in some other way. The only limit is your imagination. Go out and play three holes with one club, or pick different holes to go with different tees. Take golf out of the "normal" and get back to enjoying the experience of hitting shots and being outside—without score pressure. You'll be accessing the parts of your mind (and soul) that go far beyond pedestrian concepts like "par" and "birdie."

As we go through these components that will eventually make up the Mental Scorecard, you'll quickly see one of the main benefits of keeping this second score—especially when we're talking about the world of motivation. Immersing yourself in the task of measuring your mental focus and progress is another one of these games we've just been talking about—something that takes you out of the score-focus rut.

Case Study

My best friend, Tom, took up golf later in life, in his forties. He grew up playing tennis and skiing, and like a lot of athletes he made the transition to golf when he got older. Like the rest of us, it was easy for him to enjoy the game when he was improving—and he improved very quickly at the start. He was a 10-handicap right away, by the end of his first summer, breaking 90 and then 80 within the same month.

There's a neurological reason for feeling so good about improvement. When you experience novelty and change, it engages the dopamine pathways in the brain. That dopamine is the essence of feeling good. But when you start hitting the same kinds of bad shots over and over again and your results stagnate, you get frustrated.

It feels like a rut.

Tom whittled his handicap down to 4 but he couldn't get any lower. He wasn't having any success in the senior club championship. About four months before his next season, Tom asked me to help him.

The first thing we did was change his focus from the club championship to some fun games. He challenged himself to up-and-down games at his home course, Balboa Park Golf Course in San Diego. He played the pull-back game, where you move the ball the length of the putter away from the hole after you miss and have to convert from that distance. He also started playing Balboa Park from random tees to random greens, to change his look. I showed him an early version of the Mental Scorecard, too, and he began tracking his mental performance and prioritizing that instead of his actual score.

When it came time for the senior club championship, Tom played great and breezed his way to the title. Not only that, he shot 66 on the final day to win the regular club championship the next week, so he held both crowns at the same time—all because he reminded himself to embrace the enjoyment he got from playing instead of obsessing about results.

CHAPTER 4

Control

W HEN YOU LOOK at golf purely from a performance perspective, it really boils down to one factor.

Control.

The goal of the game is to control your ball. You're trying to hit it the right distance and direction, with the right trajectory. You're trying to make the ball go in the hole.

The control aspect extends beyond the physical requirements of the game as well. You have the power to make strategic decisions that control your fate (to a certain extent) on a hole.

And then there's the control you have—or don't have—over your emotions.

We're not machines, and golf isn't a matter of winding yourself up and clicking off shots like the USGA's Iron Byron robot. Emotions, both positive and negative, impact your golf game just as they impact your life in every other respect.

Confidence and adrenaline and joy in the right doses can all help your game. Fear and anger—and even overconfidence, adrenaline, and the euphoria that comes from hitting a great shot—can hurt your game.

To control your ball and your game, you need to be able to control your emotions.

Let's start where we left off in the last chapter: with fear.

In its most basic form, fear is easy to recognize. If you're a slicer and you step up to the tee on a hole with water all along the right side, you're probably intimately familiar with that twinge in your chest that signals you aren't comfortable.

Tournament golf turns the fear dial up even higher. When you're playing out every hole and recording your score where everybody can see it, nerves have a tendency to surface. The stakes are higher when you're playing in the semifinals of the club championship than they are if you're out for a casual round with your friends.

Crank that knob up to 12 and you're at the place where many tour players live week in and week out.

Money, titles, majors, personal glory—they're all on the line, and fear manifests itself when you're not acclimatized to your surroundings. Whatever the weakness is in your game, it'll be exposed if you aren't prepared.

As we talked about briefly in the last chapter, fear is something hardwired into the human brain as instinctual protection against danger. Throughout human history, our fear response has been finely tuned to improve our survival odds. In fact, early humans who were more fearful—and took less risks—tended to survive longer to reproduce. You and I are the result of millions of years of market research, so to speak.

Our natural fear response has become so good that it's almost too good. Biologically speaking, it's valuable to be scared of something like a truck bearing down on you. The fear response is something that would cause you to jump out of the way almost without thinking—the same way your prehistoric ancestor would have fled from a dangerous animal or a rockslide.

But biological time moves much more slowly than cultural time. There's no real survival-of-the-species reason for you to be fearful of a tight tee shot with water and out-of-bounds areas on either side, but your brain registers the fear the same way it would process physical danger. Your biology tricks you into thinking the risks are similar when they obviously aren't.

One step you can take against your own biology is to remember that your first instinctive response to fear on the golf course is an overreaction. I don't care how important the moment is. Even winning (or losing) a major championship isn't life-or-death. Life will go on if you lose a ball, drop a shot, or make a double bogey.

I helped one college golf team with this very subject by asking them to read Marcus Luttrell's book *Lone Survivor* (which has since been made into a movie starring Mark Wahlberg). Luttrell's Navy SEAL Team 10 was ambushed by Taliban forces during a mission in Afghanistan in 2005, and he was the only survivor. Luttrell made it only because he had been knocked unconscious during the course of the battle and was overlooked by enemy forces. His book recounts the story of the mission—Operation Redwing—and his escape from the Taliban despite suffering a broken back and gunshot wounds. The book certainly offers some perspective on what real fear is outside the realm of the golf course, and helps remind us that we're playing a game.

Primal emotions like fear, anger, and even joy can all disrupt what you're trying to do on the golf course. It's how we're built. You have what is essentially a one-way switch in your brain. You can process either emotion or thought. Exceed that critical mass of emotion and it short-circuits your ability to think.

You can see it happen on television almost every week on the PGA Tour—and I'm sure you've experienced it in your own game. A bad swing or a bad break leads to anger—the bang of a club on the ground, or some choice words. If you can't direct that emotion in a productive way, let it burn off, or handle it somehow, it will inevitably lead to some bad choices.

Why do you think so many fights happen in and around bars? Competitiveness—over a woman or even a sports team—increases emotion. Alcohol lowers inhibitions and clouds judgment.

Case Study

Lucinda was a terrific college player who made a fairly seamless transition to the LPGA Tour. She was consistently in the top fifty in money her first three seasons but wasn't able to close out a victory despite having two or three great opportunities to do so.

For Lucinda, anger was a much bigger issue than nerves or fear. She was an aggressive player who relished the opportunity to hit the big shot, but she often got sidetracked when making a mistake on a more mundane shot. Sometimes she would get so angry about missing the green with a wedge or three-putting from a relatively short distance that she would blow up and make a series of bogeys and double bogeys in a row and walk off with a 79 or 80.

I started working with Lucinda by describing her anger with a metaphor. If I handed her a hot coal, I asked, what would she do with it? "Drop it," she said, immediately. When I asked her why, she reflexively answered, "Because it would burn me."

It isn't productive to tell any player—tour pro or otherwise—to simply not get mad about a bad shot. We're all human, and we're going to lose our tempers from time to time. At the tour level, you're going to see some anger and frustration if a player makes what he or she considers an easily avoidable mistake. I told Lucinda it was OK to get angry, but she needed to give herself a time frame to process the anger—on the walk between that shot and the next one. I also told her caddie not to hand her the club for the next shot unless it looked like she had her emotional equilibrium back somewhere close to even.

For the rest of the season, Lucinda's results were much more consistent—and much more in line with her talent. She won her first event and signed a great endorsement deal with an up-and-coming clothing company. She did that without sacrificing the fire and competitiveness that made her such a good player in the first place—and a popular interview in the media center.

. . .

ONE OF THE beautiful things about golf is that it isn't continuous like tennis. You have the chance to recompose yourself after a bad swing and think about what you need to do next.

Part of Tiger Woods's success over the past fifteen years is his uncanny ability to channel adrenaline and even anger. He certainly has his moments of emotional outburst on the course, slamming clubs and swearing. But he's able to pare the anger and emotion down to a point where he can use it for a boost of energy and power in his shots. He's directing it in a focused way. John McEnroe was a virtuoso at this same skill in tennis.

We might not have those superpower mental skills like Tiger or Mac, but there are definitely things you can do to pull yourself together after losing your temper and get things back to a manageable level.

First, control your speed. As you get agitated, you're going to subconsciously start doing everything faster. You're going to walk faster and make hastier decisions. Change that rhythm on the walk to the next shot and slow your breathing for a minute. Time sands the edges off any emotion.

Another powerful tactic is to give yourself permission to tolerate your anger ahead of time. If you prepare for the emotion in advance, it tends not to have as strong an impact. And the reality of golf is that everybody hits bad shots. They're part of the game. Tour players want to be perfect, but it's impossible—and the perfect setup for frustration unless you're more realistic. If you're a 20-handicapper, you're going to hit some squirrely shots. You have to come into it with the idea that that's OK, and the measure of your game and your round is how you respond to those inevitable bad shots.

You can also play some practice games that will help desensitize you from the anger. One in particular that I like is breaking up practice rounds into three-hole segments. If you make a mistake within the segment, it's OK, because you're going to begin a new one soon enough.

It's important to stress that you don't have to be an emotionless robot. The key is to stay below the emotional level that blows the fuse, so to speak. Of course, this level varies from player to player, but using these techniques will help you stay in the "safe" zone whether you're a naturally fiery person or someone who is a little more reserved. Tiger is a master at this, among other things. When he hits a terrible shot, he'll often vent his anger immediately with some unprintable words. The venting works just like the term implies: It immediately blows off some of the steam.

Tiger gets hot about hitting a bad shot, but he has his reaction, takes a few angry steps, then composes himself before he moves to the next shot. Of course, the trick is to be able to allow yourself that anger and reel it back in. That *does* take some practice and self-control.

All of this advice also holds true when you do something great, like hole a bomb of a putt or hit a terrific drive. Of course you're going to be pumped and excited about executing a terrific shot. But just like with anger and fear, if you're still on that emotional high from the previous shot, you can short-circuit what you're trying to do on the next one. You can use all of the same techniques—waiting to pull the club until you've finished processing the last shot; modulating your pace between shots—that work with the negative emotions.

ANXIETY

Anxiety is related to fear in that it produces similar physical and mental responses, but it is different in that it happens without any specific or immediate external threat. If fear is the emotion you feel when you're about to hit a tee shot on that tight par-4, anxiety is what you're feeling the night before playing an important round with your boss or a prospective client. It's what tour players feel when they're sleeping on the lead on Saturday night at a major for the first time.

When anxiety hits, you start inventing worst-case scenarios and your confidence gets shaken. Uncertainty is scary, which just escalates the anxiety.

To disrupt the anxiety cycle, first remember that a little anxiety is a good thing. Those "butterflies," as Tiger Woods calls them, signal that you're in hyperalert "battle" mode. Without any anxiety, you'd be emotionally flat and uninspired. With some, you're stronger and more focused—if you can learn to embrace it. I find that simply discussing and understanding this dual effect—that anxiety is natural and good—goes a long way toward harnessing it or channeling it in a positive way.

Still, you may get into a scenario where you're feeling overwhelmed by anxiety. The idea of embracing the anxiousness isn't helping, and frankly you're just freaking out. Fortunately, modern science has discovered simple ways to use the body's own processes to ramp down the anxiety level.

If you're familiar with yoga, you probably know this breathing technique: the "yogic" or "clearing" breath. It works equally well on the golf course. Place your hand softly on your belly and breathe in through your nose to a count of four. Hold that breath and

ANXIETY-PERFORMANCE GRAPH

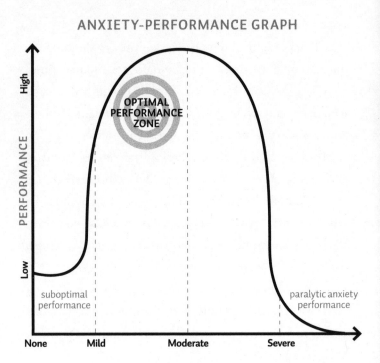

then exhale through your mouth to a count of eight. Smoothly inhale and exhale, alternating the four and eight counts through the nose and mouth. It works by engaging the vagus nerve deep in your diaphragm, which automatically short-circuits the body's fight-or-flight response. It decreases your heart rate and reduces your blood pressure.

Just as practicing your golf swing improves your form, working on your yogic breathing technique can dramatically improve your ability to handle anxiety. A swing coach watches videos to pinpoint particular angles and positions in your swing. Your heart rate variability, or HRV, is the equivalent when it comes to breathing. The greater the time interval between your heartbeats, the larger your HRV score is. And the larger your HRV score is, the easier it is to relax. A higher HRV score has been linked to lower stress, better athletic performance, and improved overall health.

There are whole textbooks on how the nervous system works, but I'll give you a brief synopsis for background. Your autonomic nervous system controls the "automatic" vital processes in your body—breathing, heart rate, some reflexes like blinking, and so on—largely without any conscious input from you. You don't walk down the street consciously willing your heart to beat each time, even though it's a muscle just like your thigh or biceps.

How your autonomic nervous system responds to a stimulus can be roughly divided into two categories: sympathetic (the fight-or-flight response) and parasympathetic (the relaxation response). By training your HRV, you're improving the performance of your autonomic nervous system's relaxation response.

One way to do that is to go to an ashram in India and devote years of study to yogic breathing techniques. If that doesn't fit your schedule, you can use one of the clever new smartphone and tablet apps that measure and train HRV. They work through a sensor that attaches to your finger. By following a series of breathing exercises to be completed at home or in a gym (or anywhere else), you make your HRV score rise. It's roughly analogous to an increase in how much you bench-press translating into ten yards more distance off the tee. Increasing your ability to handle anxiety will improve the decisions you make.

Whether you use breathing techniques like this or any other relaxation strategy, the overall point to remember is that you're ultimately looking for a feeling of preparedness. By the time you get to the golf course, you're not going to find something mechanical at the range that will fundamentally change how you play. What *can* change your performance is stretching and preparing in a way that relaxes you and gets you in a calm mental space to play.

As a young table tennis player, I happened to get the chance to talk with the legendary tennis player Pancho Gonzales. He told me about a little trick he used to relax before a match, which I adapted for use in my own table tennis career, and I've shared it with my golf clients as well. He would walk onto the court and pick the farthest seat at the top row of the stands—or the farthest tree on an outside court—and he would spend some time just concentrating on that seat or tree. It was his pre-match ritual, and it became a form of anxiety-dissolving meditation.

Homework
Visit my Web site, DrLardon.com, and click on the tab "Resources." You'll hear a customized breathing exercise created for a top Division I golf team. Download the clip and store it on your smartphone. When you get to the course before your next round, spend ten minutes listening to it before you get out of the car.

FRUSTRATION IS A natural part of golf, both in the macro and micro sense. Giving in to it is another common way players lose control. In the context of a round of golf, the difficulty of the course or the weather can certainly offer the potential for some frustration. One of the stories I shared in my previous book, *Finding Your Zone: Ten Core Lessons for Achieving Peak Performance in Sports and Life,* was about my experience with Steve Elkington at the 2007 U.S. Open. The rough was particularly brutal that year, and the slightest unlucky bounce could make the next shot virtually unplayable.

I was walking with Steve's group during an early-week practice round, and all of the players were commenting about how unforgiving the setup was. Steve hit a terrific drive right down the middle of the fairway, and it kept running on the firm fairways until it trickled just off the tightest cut. I was walking ahead, so I got to his ball before he did. It took me a few minutes to actually find it in the deep grass, and I figured he wasn't going to be pleased when he saw it.

It would have been understandable for Steve to get frustrated (or angry) about the bad break, but great players always tell themselves that those kinds of things are bound to happen. Instead of feeling that frustration, he looked at the lie with a combination of curiosity and amazement. Then he challenged himself to play a creative shot to extricate himself. He hooded a 7-iron and chopped an amazing shot out and onto the green. If he had gotten angry and hasty, he probably would have made a bad decision—or a bad swing.

Looking at the bigger picture, frustration is a common symptom of the lesson-taking process. If you're working on your game and hit a plateau, it might seem like you're never going to get better. I'm not suggesting you plug along forever working with a teacher who might not be helping you, but keep in mind that the improvement process doesn't happen in a straight line. Even with the greatest teacher in the world, you're going to have periods of improvement mixed with periods of "consolidation." As shown in the graph on page 87, you'll see a wider variety of performances early in each cycle, with your performance becoming more consistent as you master a particular level. The sequence then repeats at the next level.

If you go into the process understanding this, you're going to get less frustrated as time goes on. You're also going to learn how to deal with frustration itself—something you've probably worked on with your own kids!

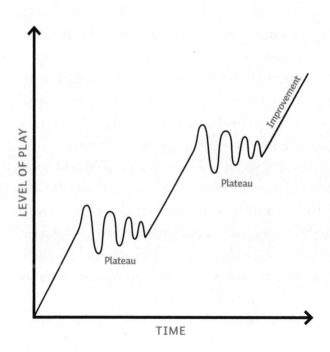

THE PRE-SHOT ROUTINE

When I was caddying for my brother at Q-school finals in 1996, I decided to do a little informal field study. I started timing the pre-shot routines of various players, and I compared the consistency of their routines with their eventual scores. My sample size wasn't huge, but I bet you aren't surprised to hear that the players who went through their routines in a consistent amount of time played the best.

I want to finish this section of the book by touching on the basics of a good pre-shot routine because I think it's the single most important element you can import into your game to take mental control.

I'm sure you've seen tour players go through their idiosyncratic pre-shot rituals—some combination of eyeing the target, stepping into the shot, and waggling the club. Pre-performance routines aren't just a part of golf. Basketball players use them when they shoot free throws. Field goal kickers go through them before the snap. Athletes in every sport use some routine to create a psychological bubble around themselves so they can block out the background noise and become fully immersed in what they want to accomplish.

Done properly, a good pre-shot routine can almost

completely banish excessive emotional arousal and anxiety.

As I watched those players at Q-school go from the comfort of the driving range to the first tee and on to the last few holes of the tournament, I could see that as they became more nervous and emotionally aroused, some players dramatically sped up or slowed down in their routines. They waggled more or less. They visualized more or less. In short, they did something completely different than when they were "comfortable."

But the players who were solid throughout the tournament had almost metronomic routines. If you watched a replay of their entire process without knowing where they stood on the leaderboard, you wouldn't know if you were watching a shot on Tuesday morning or on Sunday afternoon.

The players who struggled to go through a consistent routine got to the point where they were going to swing the club on a different routine or pattern than normal. This difference in rhythm caused tiny changes in how they actually struck the ball. It resulted in not-quite-crisp shots and missed putts. Meanwhile, the players with great routines played with beautiful rhythm—as I'm sure you've seen guys like Phil Mickelson and Tiger Woods do.

To develop your own routine, start with what you

already do under calm conditions. Play a casual round with a friend and ask him or her to track your routine at several random points during the round—on a couple of tee shots, a couple of approach shots, a couple of short game shots, and a couple of putts. What exactly did you do from the time you pulled the club to impact? How long did it take?

Assuming your routine incorporates all the elements you want (and now would be a good time to reflect on your visualization and decision-making skills), you should have a relatively consistent window of time it takes you to go through your pre-shot process.

Here's what my pre-shot routine looks like. It takes me twelve seconds to complete.

PRE-SHOT ROUTINE
Get behind ball with club
See target
Step into stance
Two waggles
Look up to see target
One waggle
Execute

The next time you watch a tour event—especially on a Sunday afternoon—make a note of what the leaders' pre-shot routines look like. Compare and contrast what they involve and how long they take. You'll see some interesting differences and similarities.

Once you've committed to a specific routine—one that feels natural—you need to practice it so that you can consistently complete it within a second or two of your "ideal" time. The best way to do that is to commit to practice sessions where you go through your pre-shot routine before every shot you hit. You're obviously going to be hitting fewer balls than normal, and it might seem like tedious work, but it will provide you with far more value out on the course than mindlessly banging out bucket after bucket of range balls.

Once your routine starts to become an integral part of the process of hitting a shot, you'll rapidly improve your ability to visualize the shot you're about to hit. You'll be able to tune in this picture in your mind much more clearly. This visualization process primes the pathways your muscles will use to fire when they actually perform the swing, and your motor function will get much more precise.

Your mind will truly control your swing.

Homework

Close your eyes and image what your pre-shot routine looks like. Picture as many small details as you can, such as when you grip the club with each hand and how many times you shuffle your feet.

Write down your pre-shot routine—from the time you get behind the ball to the time you make contact—in the box below.

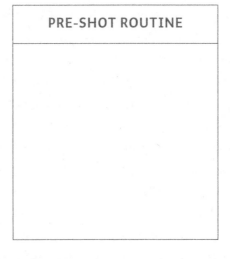

PRE-SHOT ROUTINE

Use the video camera on your smartphone to record your pre-shot routine. How close was it to what you wrote in the box? Now revise what you wrote in the box to reflect what's on the video.

Visit this box intermittently, write down your pre-shot routine in the box, and see if you have gained a clearer image of what it is you do before you swing the club. Refine this image and practice it, and through mental imagery you will improve your pre-shot routine and your ability to play under pressure.

Case Study

Andrew is one of the large group of players on the PGA Tour with a strong Christian faith. He and I haven't worked together professionally, but we've become good friends through our mutual friends. It has been fascinating to watch Andrew's career over the years, because he's had great success without standout physical skills.

Andrew has won multiple events on the PGA Tour because he's been able to gain more control over his emotions than many other players. He's been able to do that with his religious faith.

You'll hear golfers—and athletes in other sports—speak very emotionally and candidly about how their higher power guided them through a challenging situation. I'm certainly not calling into question the sincerity or validity of those beliefs. My point is simply that many golfers play better because they believe that, ultimately, they aren't completely responsible for what happens. Somebody else had a bigger plan, and that can serve as an effective pressure relief valve. Their personal egos are not as wrapped up in how they play. They have fewer expectations, and they are more relaxed and trusting. They're playing with faith, and faith kills fear. You become the conduit, and there's less ego involved.

Andrew has told me that his religious faith has put golf firmly in perspective for him as something that is a job and a means for supporting his family, not his defining characteristic. "I believe that God has a plan for all of us," Andrew said. "I'm out there playing as hard as I can, but at the end of the day my wife and kids love me if I shot 62 or 92."

If that idea dovetails with the personal beliefs you already hold, it's something you can consider for yourself. Otherwise, the technique can also work even if you don't use it in conjunction with a higher power. I hesitate to call it faith in the same sense that a religious person has faith, but great players play with what is essentially "personal faith." They worry less about bad scores on a given hole because they know from their own track record that more birdies are just around the corner.

• • •

ONE YEAR WHEN I was caddying for my brother in Q-school finals, we were paired with Tommy Armour III. The format of Q-school is unique in that it's four days of play before the cut and then two rounds to finish. On the first hole of the first round, Tommy opened with quadruple bogey 8. For most players, the wheels would have come off, but he stayed cool. To get to the weekend, you needed to be at 6 under, and he methodically worked his way back to make it on the number. Then Tommy played great on the weekend and earned his card. I remember talking to him after the last round, and he said, "I've been playing golf my whole life. I know how well I can play and what I can do. I knew I had ninety-five holes to go, and if I kept my composure, there was enough golf left out there."

Even if you don't make five or six birdies a round, you can use this same psychological profile for yourself. If you reliably shoot in the low 80s, a front nine of 46 or 47 is an aberration. Treat it as such, and remember that you're going to head back to your "average" sometime soon.

CHAPTER 5

Optimization

A MODERN SWING LESSON from a golf instructor is an amazing thing to watch. High-speed cameras, K-Vest, force plates, and computer screens are a regular part of the improvement process. You can make a swing and then come over to watch that swing on the screen with a teacher who can critique it in slow motion, examine every technical detail, and compare it to the "optimum" swing of virtually any tour player from the last thirty years.

In simple terms, it's easier than ever to see and understand what the ideal golf swing looks like.

But most players don't spend a tenth of the time "optimizing" the element of the game that has even more impact on score than the quality of the swing.

To play better, you need to optimize how you think. How do you do that?

It starts where your thoughts and moods intersect.

Your mood—your emotional state—is influenced by your thoughts. While it might feel like a good mood or a bad mood is a random occurrence, moods are driven by a variety of factors: thoughts, sleep patterns, stress levels.

When you think positively and feel good about something in your life—your relationship with your partner, your job, your golf game—your mood lifts. And in golf, when you have that elevated mood, you tend to play better. If you're thinking to yourself, *I'm hitting the ball great* or *I'm really rolling the ball well,* you're influencing your mind in a positive way. You're essentially priming yourself to continue to perform well.

As you probably suspect, the opposite is also true. If you think negatively about yourself and your game—*I just can't hit my driver* or *I can't buy a putt today*—you're influencing your mind and your game in a negative way. You're prompting more of the bad stuff.

The thought-mood link works as a cycle. In the positive performance cycle, your positive thoughts are promoting a great mood, which promotes more positive thoughts. In the negative performance cycle, the opposite is happening.

POSITIVE PERFORMANCE CYCLE

(+)
THOUGHT

I'm hitting the
ball well.

My feel around the
greens is good.

(↑)
MOOD

I'm having fun.
I'm excited.

NEGATIVE PERFORMANCE CYCLE

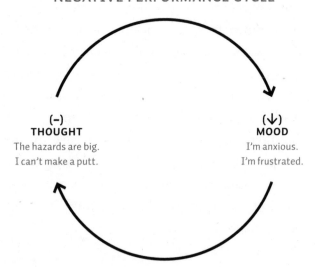

(−)
THOUGHT

The hazards are big.
I can't make a putt.

(↓)
MOOD

I'm anxious.
I'm frustrated.

Our goal here is twofold. As a player, you want to do everything you can to set yourself up in a positive performance cycle as often as possible. But negative thoughts and moods are also an inevitable part of life and golf, and you want to learn how to recognize when they're coming and head them off before they damage your score.

For years, mental health professionals have used a powerful tool called cognitive behavioral therapy (CBT) to help patients gain more control over their moods. You don't need a PhD to understand how CBT works or to implement some of its techniques.

The fundamental principle of CBT is that your thoughts—and not external things like other people, events, and circumstances—strongly determine your moods and behavior. Therefore, you can change the way you feel and act by changing the way you think, even if your external environment doesn't change.

You can choose how and what you think, which means you can choose how and what you feel.

The basics work like this: Start by noting your thoughts and use of language, and evaluate them to see if they distort the reality of your situation. If they do—and most of the time they will—you make an adjustment. You reframe your language to provide a more realistic and positive perspective. You're correcting a "thought distortion" and replacing it with "objective reality."

Case Study

Sara was a standout track athlete in high school and went on to be an NCAA champion in college. She dedicated herself to training for the U.S. Olympic trials and was one of the favorites for a spot on the Olympic team in her event, the 400-meter hurdles. But in the final race of the trials, Sara caught the last hurdle and fell. She missed making the team and was understandably disappointed and angry.

Afterward she was visibly crushed when I talked with her. "I always choke in the big ones," she said.

I waited for a minute to give her some time to compose herself, and then I asked her to think about her career record and tell me if that was really true. "Well, no . . ." she said. "I won the state championship in high school, and then the NCAAs."

"Those were pretty big ones, weren't they?" I asked her.

We talked about the result she'd just had in the trials race and her overall career, and I asked her to reconstruct her statement in a positive way, reflecting the objective reality of the situation.

She took out a notebook and wrote, "I missed making the team in my first Olympic trials, but I was right there at the end. Next time, I won't miss the last hurdle."

I asked her if she believed what she had just written. She said, "Yes, I do."

I asked her how it made her feel.

"Better. Much better."

Six months later, Sara set the U.S. record in the 400-meter hurdles, and the next year she won an important international meet. She qualified easily for the next Olympic team.

She learned from the adversity, and it helped her grow.

Homework

Think about some part of your golf game you don't like and a typical negative statement you might think or say to someone.

- In the "Statement" column, write down the comment. An example might be, "I'm a terrible putter."
- In the "Data" column, write the appropriate facts about your game. For example, how many putts do you take per round? How has that number changed over months and years?

- In the "Thought Distortion" column, make the assessment whether the facts (data) are consistent with the statement you made about your game. If the statement is accurate, check the "No" box, but if the statement is an exaggeration or distortion of the objective truth, check the "Yes" box, noting the thought distortion (as humans we almost always make some cognitive distortion).
- In the "Reframe" column, rewrite your original statement without any distortion, framing what you say in a positive way.

Take a moment and read the reframe statement you made about your game and think how it makes you feel. Ask yourself, *Does it make me feel better than my first statement did?*

Chances are it does.

Get a small notebook and make your own "thought journal" with the four columns we just discussed. Keep the notebook in your bag and make notes in it from round to round when you find yourself making negative statements or having negative thoughts. As you build a bank of examples, you'll be able to go back in the notebook and refer to how you've reframed the statements. By reading the older entries, you'll automatically trigger the positive associations that go with the new statements.

THOUGHT HYGIENE ASSESSMENT TOOL

STATEMENT	DATA	THOUGHT DISTORTION	REFRAME
		◯ YES ◯ NO	

According to the old cliché, golf doesn't build character so much as it reveals it. Of course, it's a cliché because it's true. The game is really a microcosm of who we are, because it provides such a variety of mental, emotional, and physical challenges.

I've had clients who come off the course after a tough loss and don't go through the process of metabolizing the disappointment in a productive way like Sara did in the example above. They would go on to miss four or five cuts in a row, because the thought distortion just snowballed. A bad putting day turned into "I'm a terrible putter." A few wayward drives turned into "I can't hit it with the big guys anymore." It can even happen after a *good* result. It doesn't take long for talk like "I've got this all figured out" to lead to getting comfortable—and lazy.

But as you develop some of these optimization skills, you'll start to perform a kind of thought hygiene routine just like you do on your teeth when you wake up in the morning. It isn't as much a matter of doing this major mental surgery as it is a daily awareness of where you are and maintaining this positive cycle.

Phil Mickelson is a terrific example of this. When he lost the 2013 U.S. Open, he was extremely upset, as you can imagine. Some of his first thoughts were what you would expect from a forty-three-year-old player—even one at the top of his game, as Phil is: *I let this one slip away. How many more chances am I going to have?*

If he wasn't a self-aware, resilient guy, his season would have turned out much differently than it did. We talked about the loss and whether or not it was completely under his control. Justin Rose played great golf over the last three holes, which was an important piece to remember. And statistically, Phil was playing as well as he ever had, which certainly indicated he wasn't out of chances. He had played at a high level on an extremely tough golf course. He put himself in position.

You know what happened next, at the British Open.

The ability to cleanse your mind and win a major

championship is a big, dramatic thing, but the concept of thought hygiene is just as applicable to everyday, mundane things like the weather, course conditions, and your playing partners.

To play your best golf, you want to be flexible enough to accept what the day has in store for you. Much of that acceptance comes from preparing yourself so that there aren't many surprises.

One of my favorite training stories comes from swimmer Michael Phelps, who is the most successful Olympian in history. One day his coach, Bob Bowman, sabotaged Phelps's goggles so that they would fall apart during a race. Needless to say, Phelps wasn't pleased by that. But years later, at the 2008 Olympics in Beijing, Phelps's goggles filled up with water as he jumped in the pool for the 2,000-meter butterfly final. Phelps swam the entire race blind, won the gold medal, and set a new world record. Bob's tactics helped prepare Michael for the times when conditions wouldn't be ideal.

In golf, it's one thing to tell yourself not to get frustrated by rain or wind. But to actually play through adverse conditions and embrace them, you need to practice what you preach. Follow your normal range routine no matter what the conditions, and use the time to gather information and get comfortable. It's just like any other aspect of the swing itself: If you don't practice it before you need it, you won't be able to do it when you do.

Tom Watson has one of the best records in British Open history because he embraced the wind and weather in the United Kingdom—and knew that many other players would be put off by the challenge. He knew they would play worse, leaving fewer people to challenge him. Tom saw the challenge as an opportunity and created a narrative in his mind that helped him feel positive about playing in adverse conditions. His results reinforced his positive feelings about the tournament, and he went into it every year feeling like he had a great chance to win—something he almost pulled off again at age fifty-nine in 2009.

The Watson-Cink British Open is a terrific case study for mental optimization in so many ways. I preach to my professional clients the idea that they should expect the unexpected so that they can play without being surprised. Imagine what Stewart Cink was going through down the stretch on Sunday at Turnberry. He had never won a major up to that point, which presented its own challenges. And now, as he was trying to achieve that career goal, he was in an arena even the most accomplished novelist couldn't have created out of thin air. He was going head-to-head with one of the most popular British Open champions of all time—in Scotland, where Watson is beloved. Aside from Stewart's immediate family, there probably wasn't one person within four hundred miles of Turnberry who wasn't rooting for Watson to pull off the greatest major championship victory since Nicklaus's at the Masters in 1986.

But Cink kept his composure and made a twelve-footer for birdie on the last hole, then watched Watson come in behind him. Tom ultimately bogeyed the 18th to finish second.

Cink's quest to break through in a major is a common one for tour players, and it has distinct parallels in the amateur game. We're all trying to win our own personal majors or break our particular scoring goals. I call it "climbing the ladder." You're trying to put yourself in position on the next rung time and time again to the point where you're comfortable at the higher step.

You're not on the same ladder as Stewart Cink, Rickie Fowler, or Tiger Woods, but your ladder works the same way and serves the same purpose.

I learned a lot about this ladder during my time as my brother's caddy in Q-school. The finals were at the same place for a few times in a row, but the qualifying score—what would get you out on tour the next year—kept going lower and lower. The first year, it was 9 under par, and then it was 12 and 16 under.

In the ten Q-school finals we were in together, Brad made it or missed it by one shot every single time. He was always on that bubble. That fact reinforced for him that it was always important to know where he stood in relation to the cut line and to that projected card number once we made it through. Even when I knew we were safely inside the cut line, I would try to redirect the conversation to this idea of climbing the ladder, because I wanted him to keep the accelerator down and score as low as he could.

I'm sure you've noticed the same phenomenon in your own game, even if it was wearing a disguise. If you're a 10-handicapper and you shoot 35 on the front nine, you most likely ballooned to 45 on the back, to shoot a score firmly in your comfort zone for eighteen holes.

The switch point to move up the steps of the ladder is a mind-set change. It's thinking about the target in a different way. For example, if you told me you have trouble getting started in a round and usually make two or three bogeys in the first four holes, I'd want you to change your pre-round preparation. If you incorporate some competitive games into your pre-round practice—chipping or putting for dollars with a buddy or something like that—you then go to the first tee already primed for competition and making a score.

If you're the person who shot that score five or

six shots below your handicap on the front nine, I would want you to try to play the back as if the round wasn't over at 18. If you can tell yourself you're playing twenty-seven holes, your score at the end of 18 doesn't really matter. Do that for a couple of practice rounds and you'll discover that the back nine starts to feel like a part of the same round as the beginning nine—not the "final lap," so to speak.

The last piece of the ladder puzzle involves developing that ability to continue to push the accelerator. I'm not talking about taking reckless chances and firing at every flag. It's about holding on to the mind-set that strong performances hole by hole are important to put in the bank, because you might need them later on. Invariably, when you start looking to try to "just" finish up with three pars (or three bogeys), you make the big mistake that blows up your round.

One tactic I learned years ago from a table tennis friend has a great application in golf. Danny Seemiller was one of my main rivals as a young player, and no matter how he stood in any match, he would always approach it as if he were losing. Adopting that mind-set gave him the freedom to go for his shots and stoked his competitive fire. He fought harder and finished better than he did with a more conservative mind-set. It worked for him too. He won the United States Championship five times from 1976 to 1983.

Playing those kinds of internal games with yourself is really just optimization by another name. This type of mental game occupies your mind in place of the negative thought or stimulus you're trying to erase. Do that consistently enough and you desensitize yourself to the negative or aggravating thought.

A bad pairing is a perfect example. There are probably people at your course (or job) who you don't like to play with. Either they're not friendly or they simply do something that annoys you. Maybe you're a quiet player and they like to chat, or you play very serious putt-them-all golf and they knock it around very casually. The game becomes measuring how you deal with these things. You can tell yourself, *This is my opportunity to improve my ability to play with a slow player.*

You're practicing the skill of playing in your own little world.

I'm sure you remember when Tiger Woods and caddie Steve Williams parted ways several years ago. There were some bad feelings between them, and Williams had some harsh words for the way Tiger handled the breakup.

Williams went on to caddie for Adam Scott, and in an almost theatrical development, one of their first competitive rounds as a team came when they were paired with Tiger Woods and his new caddie, Joe LaCava.

You can imagine what the vibe must have been like for five hours inside the ropes.

But Tiger has always played his game with cool detachment. His style is not to get close to his competitors and to keep personal issues from distracting his play. In psychiatry we call it "therapeutic distance," and it's certainly a style that is very effective in professional sports.

The moral of this story is that golf almost never happens under "perfect" conditions. You're playing with people you don't like, or people who play slowly, on courses that have greens that are too fast or fairways that are too tight. On tour, players have to learn to deal with spike marks, slow-playing partners, six-hour pro-am rounds, and a host of other annoyances. The sooner you embrace the idea that the fun is in testing yourself on those challenges—and not waiting for "perfect" anything—the more you're going to enjoy yourself and the better you're going to play. For a tour player, it's a matter of professional livelihood.

One of the main roles the Mental Scorecard plays is in helping you channel all of these extraneous thoughts and worries into something simpler, more focused, and easier to manage. You get caught up in thinking about the process and forget about the consequences of what you're doing.

It takes advantage of the way our minds want to work.

One interaction I had with Phil Mickelson in 2012 illustrates this point very well. After one round at the Scottish Open, Phil told me he was struggling with his game. He said he had too many swing thoughts going through his head and he needed something simple to focus on.

First I asked him what single visual image came to his mind when he thought about swinging well. He paused for a few seconds and then gave me his example.

Then I asked him if he swung the club while picturing that image, would he be doing the technical things he wanted to be doing with his swing?

He paused for another few seconds, then said yes.

I suggested he go out to the range in the morning and hit balls with one goal: to swing with that image in his mind.

He shot 64 that day.

You obviously need to use your mind to process information and make strategic decisions. Phil didn't walk around Loch Lomond that day in a haze, holding out his hand for Jim "Bones" Mackay to stick in it whatever club he thought was the right one.

Where is my target?
How far do I need to hit it?

What is the wind doing?

What kind of shot do I need to hit?

Those are just a few of the dozens of conscious and unconscious decisions that go into just one shot. But once you've made those decisions, you need to make the transition from this active-mind place to a focused, single-minded place.

All-time great Billy Casper used to tell me that he would get over the ball and think one thing: *Finish high*. It's so simple, it's genius. He went with a nontechnical thought that crowded out any of the potential negative thoughts that could creep in. Another of my favorite stories comes from playing and teaching legend Dave Stockton, who talks about a conversation he had with Byron Nelson in the 1970s about Nelson's streak of eleven consecutive wins in 1945. Byron told Dave that he played that entire stretch with one swing thought: He hit only enough balls to get loose before a round, then went out to play with that one thought, no matter what. Dave didn't bother to ask Byron what the swing thought was, because it didn't apply to his own game, but immediately took from Byron's story the bigger, more important point about clearing and focusing your mind.

Adapt that idea to suit your own game by picking a nontechnical positive thought that works as a kind of trigger. One of my players uses the idea of turning his belt buckle while swinging, while another thinks about a Magic Marker painting a yellow stripe down some railroad tracks for his follow-through.

The reason this trick works so well is that our minds can process only one conscious thought at a time. By using the Mental Scorecard—or the focusing strategies we talked about with Mickelson and Casper—you're engaging in what's called "thought substitution."

You're directing your mind instead of letting it direct you.

It's a simple and powerful tool.

If you need proof, all you have to do is try not to listen to Lady Gaga.

Believe it or not, researchers have actually investigated the phenomenon we all recognize as getting a song stuck in our heads. And they've even come up with a term for it: When you can't get "Paparazzi" or "Bad Romance" out of your head, you have what's known as an earworm. But music psychologists discovered that cognitively engaging in something else, like a puzzle or a novel, is the best way to neutralize the earworm. In the study, the key was to find a task that engaged the brain sufficiently but didn't overtax it.

Try it yourself. Pick your favorite earworm song and listen to it online three or four times in a row.

Now test this theory by doing a few Sudoku puzzles or the early-week *New York Times* crossword.

Just be sure to keep your humming to yourself.

Before we move on and talk more about concentration and focus in Chapter Six, let's have our second test.

This time I'm going to present you with ten negative statements. Under each one, I want you to write your version of a realistic and positive reframed statement. At the end, I'll give you the versions I compiled so you can compare.

1. I can't believe how bad I am out of the sand. It took me three shots to get out on the 5th hole.
2. I'm paired with my boss at the outing tomorrow. I'm playing so badly that I'm going to embarrass myself.
3. If I could play courses that only had par 3s, I could be scratch.
4. If I have to play with Jim, I'm not going to play.
5. That might be the worst shot I've ever hit.
6. He's hitting it twenty yards by me off the tee. How am I supposed to compete with that?
7. The golf pro fit me for a new driver, but I'm

not hitting it any better. It was a complete waste of money.

8. How can they charge what they charge for green fees here? Look at how bad the greens are.

9. I leave those putts short every single time.

10. She has my number. I can't beat her.

Reframed versions:

1. That didn't go well out of the sand. If I can get just a little better from the bunker, I can take a lot of shots off my score.

2. What I shoot today isn't as important as connecting with my boss and both of us enjoying ourselves.

3. What kinds of things can I learn from how I play par 3s that would apply to longer holes?

4. I'm going to score myself today on how well I immerse myself in my own game and block out distractions.

5. I almost never hit shots like that. It's so out of character that there's no sense worrying about it.

6. Let's see if I can knock it closer with my 6-iron than he can with his 8-iron.

7. What kinds of new properties does this driver have that I can take advantage of? What changes do I need to make in order to do it?

8. I bet being the greenkeeper at a daily fee course is a tough job, especially when the weather is bad.

9. I've missed the last three putts short. I am going to get the next one to the hole or just past.

10. I'm going to play better next time. If I do, I'll be satisfied. If she gets me, she gets me.

CHAPTER 6

Concentration

N THE LAST chapter, we covered the idea of "optimized thinking," the process of learning to manage your emotions and control your thoughts.

In this chapter we're going to take the next step. Once you're able to manage your emotions and you've taken control of your thoughts, how do you use those skills within the context of a round of golf? How do you pick what thoughts to use and how do you dial in the appropriate level of concentration and focus? You can do it. You just have to practice a few simple techniques.

Let's start with some definitions.

The terms "concentration" and "focus" are thrown around pretty liberally by everyone from elementary school teachers to college football coaches. I'm sure you have a general idea of what they mean: the act of applying undivided attention to a given task or subject.

But a lot of the conversation and advice I've heard on the subject of concentration misses a couple of critical components. It doesn't take into account the different types of concentration, and it doesn't offer any practical advice about how to actually "concentrate harder," whatever that means.

We're going to change that.

First, we need to differentiate between the different kinds of focus and talk about where and when each variation comes into play in golf. The differences matter, and understanding them makes your focusing job infinitely easier. Dr. Robert Nideffer devised a theory of how our attentional focus system works. It breaks attention down into two dimensions: external and internal focus, and broad and narrow focus. Different activities require different combinations of focus on those two dimensional scales.

Let me give you an example.

A Major League Baseball hitter is tasked with an extremely tough job: He has to figure out what pitch is coming out of the pitcher's hand, react to it, and decide whether or not to swing the bat. If he swings, he has to try to determine where to swing to make square contact with the ball. All of this happens in less than half a second. In terms of focus, a hitter has to concentrate on the pitcher's release point—where the ball actually leaves the pitcher's hand—to try to determine the ball's spin. The spin pattern provides a clue about whether a fastball, curve, or slider is coming.

For that part of the job, the hitter's focus is external—on a point about sixty feet away, on the mound. But when the batter decides to hit the ball, his concentration changes to internal focus—to clearing his front side or whatever other physical movement he's trying to make.

Basketball also presents great examples of broad and narrow focus. If you're a point guard bringing the ball up the floor, you need to have broad focus on the entire court in front of you. You're reading what the overall defense is doing as well as what the defender in front of you is doing. You're determining where your teammates are going and whether or not they're available to receive a pass. You're diagnosing the big picture the same way a football quarterback does just before he gets under center.

But when you're that point guard and you get fouled as you drive to the basket, you're presented with a new job at the free-throw line. You have to block out the crowd noise and ignore the screaming and waving fans directly behind the backboard. You're using narrow focus to concentrate on shooting your free throw.

Like these other sports, golf is a mixture of focus—internal and external, broad and narrow. Players run into problems both when they lose focus and when they use the wrong kind of focus for the task at hand.

Think about the makeup of your last round. If you were out there for four or five hours, how much of that time was spent actively hitting shots? Even if you count your entire pre-shot routine as being part of the shot, it's something like thirty or forty-five minutes of the four- or five-hour round.

Narrow focus is absolutely critical when you're actually in the act of hitting a shot. As you're going through your routine and then making your swing, you want to be in tune with the specific things that are happening in the little world between your head and your feet—and the contact of the ball on the clubface is the center of this world.

But what do you think happens if you try to preserve this intense, narrow focus not just for the thirty or forty-five minutes of actual shot time but for four or five hours? It would take a tremendous amount of energy, and even if you could do it, you're compromising how well you can narrowly focus at any given point during the round.

A much, much more effective use of your focusing energy is to use that narrow focus during the times it's most necessary—during shots—and transfer to wide focus when you're in between shots. In effect, you're conserving your focus "equipment" so that it can be used most effectively throughout the whole round.

WHERE TO DIRECT YOUR CONCENTRATION

BROAD	Between Shots	Executing Shots	NARROW

The first time you're able to "pulse" your attention and switch between narrow and wide focus, you'll immediately see how much easier it is to maintain your mental energy through the round. It's no different than cramming for a test in school: If you have five hours to prepare, and you spend all five grinding on the information as hard as you can, you're not going to do as well as you would if you worked for forty-five minutes and then took a fifteen-minute break. The fresher mind works better in less time; it's more effective and more efficient.

Jack Nicklaus compared his pulsed attention technique to playing an accordion. As he approached his ball, his focus would intensify and narrow, like an accordion getting squeezed. After impact, he would release his focus, like an accordion recoiling out to its open position.

Like Jack, let your focus relax after impact and broaden to consider both your overall strategy and the "extraneous" things that make golf so wonderful: the social element, the outdoors . . . Then you can repeat the cycle as you approach the next shot.

Case Study

I met Marcus when he was playing in a U.S. Open qualifier with another client of mine. The two guys were friends, and we had dinner together early in the week. Marcus shared that he struggled to close out rounds on a strong note. He said he just felt like he was out of gas on 17 and 18. After a few minutes of conversation, it was clear to me that he was simply mentally exhausted by the time he came down the stretch. He was grinding very hard, using narrow focus to essentially spend five hours with blinders on. The effort it took to block everything out day after day was giving him tension headaches.

The next day, before his practice round, Marcus and I sat down and mapped out a plan for using narrow and wide focus and how to transition between the two.

Wide focus flows through the environment. You're scanning, taking everything in. All of your senses are engaged. You're feeling your feet brush the grass, and you hear the wind in the trees. You're smelling the grass and the food cooking at the concession stand. Maybe your playing partner makes a comment about somebody in the gallery or asks you about the basketball game last night. You're not hyperfocused, just aware of your surroundings and where you stand.

As you get closer to your ball, you start the transition back to narrow focus. It's where you start the Pre-Shot Pyramid we've been establishing in this book. If you're playing with a caddie, you both go through your calculations. How far do you have to your target? What shot are you going to hit? Go through your pre-shot routine. See the shot. Feel the shot.

Then, lastly, hit it.

Marcus went out and played his practice round using this technique of alternating between wide and narrow focus. It took him a few holes to really commit to the process and the experiment, but at the end of the day he was thrilled with the results. He decided to make the leap and play his qualifying rounds that way.

U.S. Open sectional qualifying is some of the most competitive golf out there—a hundred talented players going for just a few spots in the U.S. Open. Marcus played great both days, sinking a thirty-footer on the last hole to earn a spot in the Open. He followed that up with some terrific play on the Nationwide Tour the rest of that summer, and he earned a PGA Tour card at Q-school finals that fall.

You can think of the narrow-versus-wide spectrum as covering your location on the golf course. The internal-versus-external spectrum pertains to whether you're learning a skill or using it.

I call it *training* versus *trusting*.

Training mode is just what it sounds like: You're learning how to do something—whether it's something basic like holding the club or a more sophisticated piece of swing advice from your teacher. In the ideal training scenario, you're completely internally focused. You're paying attention to what you want your body to do and how close you're coming to actually doing it. You go over what you've been taught and think about what you're doing—that is, you practice with purpose and intensity. Your intention is to optimize your technique and, through lots of practice, automate your swing. Then, when you play, you go with your automated swing. If you're hitting a cut that day, then hit the cut. If you need to learn to hit a draw, experiment with that shot when it's training time—not on the course.

In *trusting* mode, your focus moves away from what you're doing with your body and toward what is happening in your environment. Where is the target? What is the best strategy to reach the target? What are the hazards and safe landing spots? You're accepting your physical game for what it is and concentrating on using it in the most effective way.

But many amateur players never really get out of training mode. They go to the first tee of a real, competitive round with a new swing tip or temporary swing "Band-Aid"—in hopes that it will stick for the day. If you're on the fourth or fifth tee thinking about the different backswing move you're going to make to try to stop slicing it, you're in training mode, not trusting mode.

GOLF'S TWO MENTALITIES

TRAIN	TRUST
PRACTICE FACILITY	**GOLF COURSE**
—	—
Experiment with technique and swing changes.	Think only about strategy.
—	—
Work on your lessons, use video, and play creative games.	Use either NO swing thoughts or just one simple swing thought.

Train your swing when you practice. *Have fun and be creative.*

Trust your swing when you compete. *Have patience and be disciplined.*

My dad is a great example of what happens when you play (or practice) on the wrong side of those two spectrums. He absolutely loved the game, but he never got better than the 18 to 22 handicap range. It wasn't from lack of effort or lack of interest in competition. In fact, he might have been *too* competitive. My dad's problem was that he had a narrow, external focus all the time, whether he was hitting shots, walking from shot to shot, playing, or practicing. He never approached his swing in a mechanical way, so he was never able to beat his big swing flaw: falling back at impact. He ground away extremely hard every minute when he played, as if he could somehow *will* himself to a better score. By using *all* of his focus energy *all* of the time, he never had ideal focus *any* of the time.

My dad's focus diagram would look like this:

EXTERNAL

	Between Shots Executing Shots Practicing Competing

BROAD   **NARROW**

INTERNAL

Compare that to what an ideal diagram would look like.

GOLF'S OPTIMAL
FOCUS DIMENSIONS

EXTERNAL

Competing

BROAD   Between Shots   Executing Shots   **NARROW**

Practicing

INTERNAL

Whether you're practicing or playing, your focus is narrow when you're actually hitting shots and wide when you're in between shots. It's an important point, because you're going to get more from your practice routine if you pulse your attention, as Jack described, just as you would when you're out playing a round. By relaxing and broadening your focus just after impact, you're both gaining more information by truly seeing the ball in flight and studying what it does downrange, and giving your brain the space and time to integrate the skills you're practicing. Mindless repetition doesn't serve any purpose except to kill time—or to groove bad habits.

Case Study

The first year Cal was a fully exempt player on the PGA Tour, he went through a stretch where he really struggled with his driver. That wasn't a normal thing for him—he's always been a terrific ball striker. But Cal had gotten caught up in thinking about the mechanics of his swing, and he couldn't hit the ball like was used to doing.

Cal wasn't somebody who had worked a lot with teachers, but he decided to reach out to a high-profile instructor for help. This teacher had already helped more than a dozen top-ten players over the last decade and was extremely well respected.

The tour was on the Texas swing at the time, and the teacher asked Cal to meet him out on the Galveston Island beach, just south of Houston. After a few minutes of chitchat, the teacher asked Cal to tee up twenty balls in a line on the hard sand. Cal did, and the teacher simply said, "Hit 'em."

Cal proceeded to crush all twenty drives dead straight, about three hundred yards into the Gulf of Mexico.

After Cal hit the last one, he looked over to the

teacher, waiting to hear some critique. The teacher paused for a few seconds, then asked, "What's the problem? You seem to be hitting it pretty good to me."

Cal's first reaction was to feel a little defensive. "I guess it's not so easy when there's trouble on the right and left," he said. "It's easy here. My target is the water. I just get up and swing it."

"Exactly," the teacher said. "Go swing like you're trying to hit into the Gulf of Mexico."

Cal started hitting his driver great again right away. The teacher had helped him clear his mind and start playing with trust again. He had helped him move his focus from internal to external.

Homework

Think about the four components we've just discussed: narrow and wide focus, and internal and external focus. On the following diagram, note where your focus is when you are:

1. Executing your shot
2. Walking between shots
3. Competing for score
4. Practicing and working on technique.

Now mark your assessments in the following diagram: (1) Executing your shot, (2) Walking between shots, (3) Competing for score, (4) Practicing and working on technique.

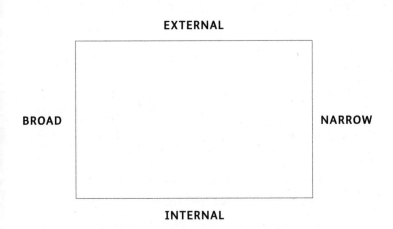

Does your diagram look like the optimal golf focus diagram? If not, pay attention to where your focus is when you are on the course and on the range and see if you can't improve your diagram.

NICKLAUS WAS ONE of the first players to talk extensively about using visualization and imagery to improve his concentration. Back in the 1970s, he talked about how he never played a shot—even in practice—without having a full picture in his head of what he wanted the ball to do. The series of images began with one of the ball sitting specifically in the spot where he intended it to finish—either in the fairway or on the green—and then "rewound" to show the full shot with a kind of tracer outlining its trajectory. It's something almost all tour players do now as a matter of routine—and a technique you can easily copy.

As we talked about earlier in the chapter, creating an image in your mind before you play has real performance benefits in neurological terms. You're priming the exact mental pathways your brain will be using to fire your muscles during a real shot. In a sense, you're practicing the shot without actually performing it.

To produce the most realistic and effective mental images, it helps to understand the different domains those images occupy in your mind—visual or kinesthetic (feel based)—and which kind you naturally respond to best.

Visual images are just what you would imagine them to be. They're essentially videos or movies that you see in your mind's eye. For example, your teacher tells you that you're bowing your left wrist in the backswing, and the club is laid off and flat at the top. That piece of information—plus a look at the teacher's video monitor—might give you a very visual image of what you're doing, as well as what you need to do to fix the swing error.

Kinesthetic images can have visual components to

them—like the bowed wrist we talked about above—but are more about the feel of what you're trying to do. Using the example above, the instructor might say that you want to feel your wrist staying flat and firm at the top of the backswing.

Your other senses can also contribute to the generation of imagery as well. Sound can be very helpful when you're working on rhythm and tempo in your swing. Something as simple as the beat of a familiar song can help remind you to maintain your routine and swing at a certain pace. Smell and taste can connect you to the memory of a relaxing or energizing experience. One player I worked with triggered her pre-shot routine with a sip of sports drink. I'm sure she's built an association with the coldness and taste of the drink that helps her click into her narrow-focus place. There's no question you draw subconscious mental comfort from the sameness of how you start.

Players often ask me what kinds of visual or kinesthetic images they should use. I'm happy to give examples—and I do at the end of this chapter—but I encourage you to go out and experiment with a wide variety of different images. On the visual side, try picturing shots both from your own "player's-eye" perspective and in the same way you'd watch a full-body image of yourself on video. In terms of feel images, try "golf-related" feels that flow with the things you're trying to do in your swing, but also experiment with non-golf-feel images, like swinging a hammer or crushing an egg with your foot. The players I coach all respond differently to different types of imagery. The best image is the image that works best for you.

Case Study

Robert is a multiple winner on the PGA Tour and is well-known for his shot making and creativity. He was successful right out of college, earning his card in his first try at Q-school and winning his first event within two years.

After finishing second in a major championship, Robert had the opportunity to sign a lucrative equipment deal with a new manufacturer. He had been using his previous brand of clubs since his college days, but the new manufacturer offered him five times as much money annually to play with their full line of equipment. Robert saw it as an opportunity to take some of the financial pressure off, allowing him to play fewer events the next season.

Robert's new equipment company took him through their process of club fitting, and his new irons were essentially identical to his previous ones. The new driver was more of a departure, and even though the numbers on the launch monitor indicated he was hitting the new club longer, higher, and straighter, Robert just didn't feel as comfortable with the new driver as he did with his old one. He loved the driver head, but didn't think the shaft felt right—even though the launch monitor suggested it was a good fit.

After a couple of months of tinkering with the new club, he decided to put it in play at the beginning of the next season, even though he wasn't completely sold on the feel.

In the first tournament of the season, Robert's driving average increased by nearly twenty yards from the previous season, but he made a triple bogey after hitting a tee shot out of bounds and ended up shooting 77. Another bad tee shot in the second round led to a double, and he shot 75 to miss the cut by miles.

Another two-hour session on video with his instructor didn't reveal any swing issues, but Robert just didn't feel good with the driver.

After another frustrating missed cut, he and I met early in the week at the next tour stop. He told me he was walking into every tee shot thinking about the driver and worried that he was going to hit a bad hook.

Robert's caddie and I got together later and I asked him to do me a favor. I wanted him to take the driver to the manufacturer's on-site rep and ask him to replace the shaft with an identical one but with no label on it. The caddie's job was then to tell Robert that they had found an identical shaft to the one in his old driver and that he'd probably have a lot better luck with this one.

At his range session before his Wednesday pro-am round, Robert took the doctored driver and gave it a couple of careful swings. He hit some towering shots with just a hint of a fade.

"Feels different," he said.

After twenty or thirty minutes of practice with the new club, Robert said he could feel himself moving back to his original routine and focus before each shot. A strong feel player, Robert had always described his imagery for hitting draws and fades as very specific kinesthetic sensations in his hands. He wouldn't use words so much as he would demonstrate with his hands how he would hold off his release slightly for a fade or turn his hands over a bit more to make the ball draw.

We finished the practice session with a drill I like to use with tour players. Just before it's time to pull the trigger, I'll call out a shot shape. The goal is for the player to simply react to my call, see it in his mind's eye, and shape the shot without too much analysis or overthinking.

Robert took what was essentially the same driver and shot four rounds in the 60s to finish in the top five that week. He had another strong season and retained a great relationship with the new club company.

Homework

During your next round, experiment using imagery in your pre-shot routine every time you hit a shot. On some shots, use visual imagery.

Some examples (but please feel free to experiment with your own):

- Seeing the shot from impact to landing point with a vivid tracer line
- Using guide points on the grass or background to frame the shape of a shot
- Picturing the spot on the circumference of the cup where the ball will actually enter on a putt.

On others, use kinesthetic imagery.
Some examples:
- Holding the club like you're holding a bird: securing it but not strangling it
- Unhinging the wrists at impact like you're pounding a nail.

Record the results of your shots using the different types of imagery. What specific images worked well or not as well? What kinds of imagery, visual or kinesthetic, worked well or not as well? Was one image or type more successful than the others? Did this surprise you?

The Mental Scorecard helps you rate yourself on how well you're creating the desired image before you hit a shot. The more you practice, the better your mental imagery will get.

Experiment in this way from time to time—once a month is a good interval—to get more feedback on both what you're choosing to visualize and how well you're making the mental pictures you do choose.

GOING BACK TO the analogy of learning how to drive a car, you've picked up how to move the steering wheel, use the pedals, and shift the gears. You also know where the mirrors are and where you need to look to see them. But when it's time to merge onto the expressway for the first time, you don't do all of these things in some random order.

You need a plan.

CHAPTER 7

Mental Plan

IMPROVING YOUR MENTAL performance is just like any other "noble" goal: Whether you're trying to think better, swing better, get in shape, or organize your life, making the decision to try to improve is a giant first step.

But just because you want to do it—and just because you're *trying*—doesn't mean you're going to be productive.

Activity doesn't equal progress.

All of the professional athletes I work with are immensely talented, driven individuals. Just the fact that they're willing to put ego aside and come to somebody for some guidance is a strong indicator that they're motivated to take action.

The first time we sit down for a get-to-know-you

consultation, I ask them two questions. They're both simple.

First, why do you want to improve your mental game?

Those answers come fast, and they're mostly what I would predict. A golfer wants to get to the next level: the tour itself, a victory, better performance in majors. A runner records great times in practice but can't translate those times into performance when it matters. A field goal kicker's job is on the line every week and he needs to learn how to manage that pressure.

The second question stops them.

What is your plan?

To start with, most professional athletes are genetic freaks. Many times, they've never needed a plan up to that point, because they've always been able to succeed with raw talent. Even in the sports where the mind plays as big a part as the body—like golf or show jumping or playing quarterback—players come to me when what they're doing isn't working anymore and they don't know how to fix it.

The world-class athletes I work with don't want to hear it, but in this way they're just like you and me.

If you want to improve something—whether it's your swing, your diet, or your mental game—you have to have a plan.

I don't care if you're trying to make the PGA Tour

for the first time, trying to win a major championship, or hoping to break 90 for the first time this summer. Practicing mindlessly and failing to evolve and adapt your game based on your performance is a losing proposition. Any success you have will be pure luck, and awfully hard to replicate.

I tell my clients they can play two kinds of golf: hacker golf or smart golf.

HACKER GOLF

The hacker's dominant characteristic is that he or she doesn't approach the game with any kind of structure. See if you can identify yourself in either of these two composites.

1. You're a decent player who has a good hole here and there, but your blowup holes keep you from ever reaching your scoring goals. You've been hounded by the same ball flight problem for ten years—a big slice—but you haven't been able to cure it at the range. You know that you could fix it with lessons and perseverance, but you don't get around to doing much more than blasting large buckets of balls downrange, aiming at nothing in particular. Every time you play, you walk onto the tee knowing you're probably going to slice it but are still angry every time it happens. You're

a consistent player, but not in the good sense. You consistently shoot scores five or ten shots worse than you could be recording.

2. You're an avid player who loves the game, and you spend good money every year on new equipment, golf trips, and lessons. But you're never satisfied with your swing. You take tips you read in magazines, see on television, and hear from playing partners and haphazardly incorporate them into your swing. If they don't work, you toss them out after a week or two. Your ball position and grip change from week to week, and you're always using a different swing thought. Every time you play a competitive round, you're standing over the ball, thinking about a checklist of physical moves you need to make to hit a great shot. On a few occasions, when your swing thoughts and compensations match up, you play a very good round and shoot a score five shots better than your handicap, but mostly your results are spotty.

Whether you're a pounder (as described in the first example) or a tinkerer (as described in the second example), you have no chance of consistently playing your best golf unless you get a plan and change your habits.

SMART GOLF

When you decide to play smart golf, you're committing yourself to taking positive and productive steps toward improvement. That doesn't always happen in a straight line, but you have the patience to see the big picture—and endure some short-term struggle.

Your internal radar probably pings when you hear a commercial—or an instructor—promise an instant fix. And it should. The only way to integrate a new technique completely is to practice it consciously until it can be transferred into the subconscious part of the mind.

I like to equate the process to the one a computer uses. A computer has RAM memory and a hard drive. RAM memory is the active, operating memory that grinds through current tasks. The hard drive is where the great bulk of information is stored long-term.

The more tasks you can relegate to your own "hard drive," the better you're going to play. You'll be able to use your RAM to handle the competitive stresses and decisions that go with playing, while your swing operates from the hard drive.

How the brain handles that transition is equal parts complicated science and mystery, but in basic terms your brain gets stronger when you learn new material.

It develops more robust synaptic connections, which are essentially the pathways on which chemical and electrical signals pass. These synapses relay information more efficiently, so your brain doesn't have to work as hard. As more and more neurons establish connections with each other, you need less and less conscious effort to complete a given task, like hitting a golf ball, driving a car, or speaking a different language.

There is a vast body of research out there on motor learning and the different ways and speeds that people acquire new skills. That's another book for a different day. But in general terms, the ultimate goal is to improve your skill set to the point that your swing is mostly automated, which gives you the luxury of swinging instinctively and without thought when you're out on the course.

To do that, you need goals.

GOAL SETTING

Why do you play golf?

That might sound like a throwaway question, but it really isn't.

Do you play because you like to be outside for a

few hours with some friends and maybe get a little exercise? Are you OK with the quality of your game the way it is?

I don't ask this to make some kind of judgment. Unless you're on one of the professional tours (or trying to get there), golf is a hobby. It's something you choose to do with your free time, hopefully because you enjoy it. It's up to you to play for your own reasons. If you're not "serious" about the game, one of the first freeing things you can do is embrace that fact and resolve to go out and have a good time. It doesn't make sense to beat yourself up about bad shots if you haven't dedicated time to practice. Again, I'm not criticizing that approach. It's just healthier to accept it for what it really is.

But if you want to improve—if you want to become a smart golfer—you need to build a set of specific, clear, productive goals toward that end. When I say "productive," I mean an appropriate mix of *process-oriented* and *results-oriented* goals, both *short-term* and *long-term*—ones that are attainable without being too easy.

Goals are important because they form the backbone of a positive feedback loop—one of the most effective tools you can use to stimulate the human brain. If you set clear, specific, productive goals and you improve in a measurable way toward those goals, your motivation to continue to improve increases. The more motivated you get, the harder you work—and the more goals you're able to reach.

Picture yourself as the subject in this next example. You're a pretty good player—a 12-handicap—but you aren't confident with your chipping or putting. A cursory analysis of your practice time shows that you're doing virtually no work on those weak parts of your game.

One of your goals for the upcoming season is to improve your chipping and putting. Your first *process-oriented* goal is to spend at least 50 percent of your practice time on those two areas. You devote your time in the *short term*, over the next two months, to the process of improving your putting and chipping, working on the mechanics of those shots with help from your instructor.

Once you've spent those weeks working on improving your technique, you develop a *long-term* goal for the rest of your season that is *results oriented*. You decide that you want to get up and down at least 60 percent of the time from thirty yards and in, and you want to average thirty putts per round or less. By the end of the year, you hope to have reduced your handicap to 8.

It is important to note here that statistics—up-and-down percentages, putts per round, and even handicaps—are unquestionably useful, but they need to occupy a healthy place in your overall scheme of goal setting. You can really improve if you use them to confirm what you're feeling about your game and show you interesting trends, but if you live and die by statistics, they can get into your head to an unhealthy degree.

Players at every level typically make the mistake of loading up on results-oriented goals: win a tournament, cut a handicap by five strokes, finish in the top fifty in money, qualify for the championship flight of the club championship. It's OK to have some of those results-oriented goals, but having that mix of process goals is crucial to overall success—and something the Mental Scorecard really helps you accomplish.

Lee Janzen's goal-setting process is simple and elegant. He plays by a three-quarter rule. He's trying to hit three-quarters of the fairways and three-quarters of the greens and make three-quarters of his putts inside ten feet. If he accomplishes those goals—and records a good score on his Mental Scorecard—he feels like the results are going to take care of themselves.

Picking an appropriate time horizon and difficulty level for your goals can also trip you up. If you thrive on the organization of having daily tasks, it's perfectly acceptable to have a set of goals for the day, like committing to forty-five minutes of practice with the driver. You just want to make sure you bracket those daily goals with some mid-term goals that cover a few weeks or a month, and longer-term goals that cover a year. If all of your goals are far into the future—say, a year out—it's hard to push yourself that entire time to take the hundreds of small steps required to achieve a big goal. Conversely, if your goals are always in a su-pershort time frame, you're going to struggle with the overall direction of your improvement.

Case Study

It sometimes takes a few years, but PGA Tour players develop the understanding that the season is a grind and that it's nearly impossible to be "up" for every event. Phil Mickelson deals with this fact by building his schedule so that it accommodates all of the things he wants to accomplish in the season both personally and professionally.

In the preseason and early part of the schedule, Phil has very process-oriented goals devoted to things like working on different mechanical aspects of his swing and dialing in any new equipment he might be putting into play. Majors are obviously a big focus for him, so he optimizes his schedule before Augusta to both maximize his chances to win tournaments and to set himself up for a great performance at the Masters. He wants to be seeing and hitting shots he's going to use at the Masters before he actually gets there.

Phil altered his process for achieving the goal of being more competitive in the 2012 British Open: He went more than ten days early to play in the Scottish Open first—both to adjust to the turf conditions in the UK and to completely acclimate to the eight-hour time zone change before the Open Championship.

Even if you aren't playing twenty-five events a year and flying all over the globe like a tour player, this concept of mapping out your practice and trying to peak at certain times of the year is certainly applicable. If you live in a place where the weather keeps you from playing for a few months, that's a great time to get started on fitness or instruction goals you have for the season so that you hit the ground running when spring finally breaks.

If you play in an important event every year—your own personal "major championship"—you can build your goals and practice plan for the year to give yourself enough time to both develop any new skills you need and integrate those skills on the course.

MANY OF THE Olympic athletes I train arrange their goals in tiers according to time frame and difficulty level. They have goals that they need to stretch to attain, like a personal best time, and also goals that will require an almost superhuman effort. The prize in the sky is an Olympic medal, but on the way to that they have team trials and world championships. To get there, they have a variety of weekly, monthly, and yearly goals that establish a baseline level of physical conditioning and that get them where they need to be in terms of technical improvement.

The thought process and goal process for a prospective Olympic high jumper has some interesting and useful parallels for the golfer. The jumper has a number he or she wants to get to: a certain height. In practice, what number is he or she actually jumping—and is that number good enough? If it is, how does he or she transfer that practice performance into performance when it counts, at the world championships or Olympic trials? It's a lot like the process you go through in golf: mastering a certain shot on the range and figuring out how to translate that into on-course performance.

Setting your target for something like a spot on the Olympic team is truly an ambitious goal. That might not be an issue for somebody who has almost superhuman talent, but you and I are going to get the best results if we build a set of goals that have attainable intermediate steps and top-end achievements that are on the hard side but definitely possible to attain.

For example, if you're a 20-handicapper who struggles with chipping, developing a 100 percent conversion goal for an up-and-down game is going to be a recipe for frustration. You'll quickly realize that you'll never get to 100 percent, and you'll become discouraged and give up. What we're trying to do here is maximize motivation in order to speed up the acquisition of skill.

A good instructor is a great asset at this point in the game. He or she can help you define success at your level. If you're working on your sand game, improving your success at just getting out of the bunker from 30 percent of the time to 80 percent of the time is a massive win. Once you're able to get out 80 percent of the time, you can pick the next goal: trying to get a certain number of shots inside a ten-foot circle around the hole. If you're on tour, the parameters are different. If Phil Mickelson doesn't get up and down from greenside bunkers more than 70 percent of the time, he's not pleased with his performance.

Case Study

Sean was an extremely talented player on the PGA Tour who had won three events in his first five or six years but was in danger of losing his card. One of his college friends was a track athlete who had worked with me on his way to a spot on the Olympic team, and the friend had suggested that Sean give me a call.

We met on the Tuesday before an event in California, and I asked Sean my standard first two questions: Why do you want to improve your mental game? And do you have a plan?

His first answer came quickly. He said he felt like he was wasting his talent. The second answer came fast too. He said he had never done anything besides go out and play golf. His college coach was his de facto instructor, but he mostly just watched Sean hit balls to warm up before a round. It wasn't his fault Sean was struggling—Sean wasn't very receptive to instruction. He had always relied on his athleticism and length off the tee.

The first thing we did, ten minutes into the conversation, was to put everything on the table. I asked Sean if he was doing any physical conditioning. What did his practice routine look like? Was he analyzing any of the statistics the PGA Tour keeps through ShotLink? What aspects of the game motivated him?

Sean's answers were both pretty grim and encouraging. Grim because he basically said everything you would hope a professional athlete wouldn't say. He didn't train. His practice routine was pretty much random and predicated on how close to his tee time he decided to get to the course. He had a passing familiarity with where he stood on some of the PGA Tour stats, but the one number he seemed to care about most was how he fared in a few standing Tuesday morning money games with some other pros.

The encouraging part was that even though Sean was failing himself in this important facet of life as a professional, he had still seen some success on the course. He was a talented player, but one who desperately needed a plan.

The first thing Sean and I did was agree that he needed to make a commitment to three coaches. I took him on as a client. He also needed to connect regularly with a trainer to build a fitness program. And he needed to make an up-front financial commitment to a swing instructor so that he would be incentivized to take the advice seriously.

We sat down and developed a notebook page of goals for his season. In the near term, one goal was to get to the gym five days a week. Another goal was to play three eighteen-hole practice rounds at an event site where he concentrated on potential pin locations—not betting with his friends. We also set a few results-oriented goals tied to statistics, like getting into the top 25 percent of the total driving category, and to reduce his putting average by a shot.

In the early run, the changes were clearly a shock to Sean's system. The trainer and instructor broke down his body and swing, and it took two or three months for him to see consistent results. But by the end of the summer, Sean was playing much better—and he looked like a completely different guy.

One of the side benefits of improved physical fitness is that it helps you process information more efficiently. Getting in shape made it easier for Sean to think better and to stick to his new plan.

He came close to winning again in the fall, just missing a birdie putt on the 18th hole that would have gotten him into a playoff with one of the top five players in the world. He missed keeping his card by a few thousand dollars, but, energized and fit from his new regime, he played great at Q-school finals and easily got his card for the next year.

Sean didn't slack off in the off-season, either. He dedicated his time to working with his teacher and started the next year fast, with a win and three top-tens in his first ten starts. He's now comfortably in the top fifty of the world rankings.

THE SIMPLEST WAY to organize all of these ideas into a useable template is to create what I call a goal-setting matrix. It places your goals into an at-a-glance format that's easy to follow—and small enough to tuck into your bag.

Say you have three result goals for this coming year:

1. Break 80 for the first time.
2. Reduce your handicap to 7 or less.
3. Win the first flight of the club championship.

Each of those goals needs a specific time frame attached to it. You're likely to break 80 first, reduce your handicap second, and win the club championship last.

Now ask yourself what you need to do to achieve your goals. The first element might be better chipping skills. The second element might be improving your mental game. The third might be playing in as many competitive events as possible to get yourself tournament tough.

These pieces are all *process-oriented,* and it's engrossing yourself in the process that produces the result. A summary of what this would look like on a goal-setting matrix sheet is on page 156.

Homework

Now it's your turn. Write down what you consider to be the strengths and weaknesses in your game. Ask yourself what three realistic goals you can achieve in your next season. Then ask yourself what you need to do to achieve each of those goals. Using the empty goal-setting matrix box on page 156, write the result

GOAL-SETTING MATRIX

	PROCESS	RESULT	
SPECIFICITY Allow creativity and autonomy	Increase short-game practice	Break 80	Short Term
	Improve mental game— work with Mental Scorecard	Lower handicap to 5 or less	Intermediate Term
	Play as many competitive events as possible	Win club championship	Long Term

goals in the result column and the way in which you are going to get there in the process column. Periodically review and revise your goal-setting matrix. It's a great way to keep you on task!

GOAL-SETTING MATRIX

	PROCESS	RESULT	
			Short Term
			Intermediate Term
			Long Term

CHAPTER 8

Building the Pre-Shot Pyramid

Y OU'VE LEARNED WHAT skills make up the individual blocks of the Pre-Shot Pyramid. And you're on your way to mastering those skills individually.

The blocks of the Pyramid interlock to form not just the basis of your pre-shot routine but the basic foundation of your physical and mental approach to each shot.

Once you learn how to use the core components together, everything you do will pull you toward the ultimate result: hitting well-planned, well-executed shots with a focused, clear mind.

Let's talk about how to do that.

The physiology of the human brain is still a mystery in some ways, but we do know some basic facts. Your brain is divided into halves, or hemispheres.

The *left brain* is considered to be the center of logic and linear thinking. Your language, counting, and decision-making abilities live there. When David Toms laid up short of the water from 235 yards on the last hole of the 2001 PGA Championship, he was using every bit of his left-brained logic and decision-making power. He decided his best play to make par was to count on his strong wedge game. He hit sand wedge to twelve feet, made the par putt, and beat Phil Mickelson by a shot.

Jack Nicklaus is the prime example of a player who earned his status as an all-time great with left-brain play. He made logical decisions, played to his strengths, and let other players beat themselves. In the women's game, Annika Sörenstam clearly read from Jack's playbook. She compiled one of the finest careers in LPGA history playing an almost ruthlessly calculating, logical game.

On the other side, the *right brain* is considered to be the home of emotion, artistry, and imagination. When Tiger Woods famously holed that chip with 90 degrees of break at the 2005 Masters—and celebrated with caddie Steve Williams afterward—he was channeling his right-brain creativity. Mickelson and Seve Ballesteros are two other prime examples of players who achieved greatness with right-brain play.

Your next logical, left-brained question is probably this: Should I play left-brain or right-brain golf?

The answer is both and neither—and it's just as true for you as it was for those seemingly one-side-dominant players we just talked about.

You want to use your logical brain to figure out what shot you are going to hit, then use your creative brain to get a feel for the shot. When it's time to actually make your swing, you move to what I call the "know brain," or the gap between thoughts. We're going to talk more about that in a minute.

The job of the Pre-Shot Pyramid is to help you manage these transitions and make them seamlessly.

PUTTING THE BLOCKS TOGETHER

Your time on the golf course can be divided into two segments. The first segment starts when you get to your ball and initiate the process of determining what shot you're going to hit. That segment lasts until you've hit the shot and seen what the result was. The other segment is made up of the time from the end of the last shot to the beginning of the next shot's initiation sequence.

Plenty of the information we've discussed in *Mastering*

Golf's Mental Game applies to the time between shots, when you need to maintain that wide focus and positive approach. Here, we're going to focus on that first segment, from shot selection to shot execution—the nuts and bolts of the Pyramid and how to use it to produce that ideal shot.

The first floor of the Pyramid is the most straightforward and logical—which makes sense, because it requires the use of the left/logical side of your brain.

STEP ONE: CALCULATE

When you get to your ball, fire up your mental computer—and that of your caddie, if you're using one—to begin the intensive process of picking the best shot for your circumstances. Factor in distance, wind, temperature, elevation, and potential hazards before identifying the shot you want to hit.

Other questions that can pass through your mind involve your own body, not the external conditions. How are you hitting the ball today? Are you hitting shots your normal distance? Longer? Shorter?

All of these calculations inform your risk assessment. What club selection, shot shape, and landing point provide the most reward with the least risk? A tour player has thousands of hours of experience with this process, and he or she still takes methodical care. You should take at least as much care and probably more—and do it with every club in the bag, from driver to putter.

I walked inside the ropes with one of my tour clients during a practice round at a major championship a few years ago and had the opportunity to watch the club selection process firsthand, over and over. The caddie provided the player with three yardages—to the front of the green, to the flag, and to the back edge of the green—then gave the player what he considered the "ideal" number to fly the ball.

That began the process in the player's mind of picturing the ideal shot shape for the target, distance, and wind. The player might have 162 yards to a back middle flag, and the options are to hit a slightly drawing 9-iron or relatively straight 8-iron. If the wind is from the left, he could play a drawing shot that would hold against the wind. If the pin is on a shelf that drops off left of the hole, he can start the shot at the left edge of the green with a slight fade and ensure that even a shot that misses slightly right of the hole will still be on the correct tier.

STEP TWO: CREATE

You might be saying to yourself that there's no point in thinking with that level of detail if you can't execute with a tour player's precision.

PRE-SHOT PYRAMID

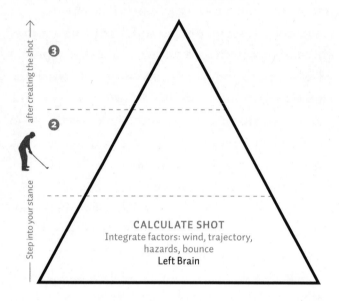

I disagree.

By going through this kind of logical, step-by-step process, you're giving your mind so much more material to use as you build your ability to visualize the shot you want to hit. You won't see the shot as the tour player's 162-yard, slightly drawing 9-iron. You'll see it as your own 7-iron with five yards of fade—with the exact start point, landing spot, and curve in flight you want to produce.

You might not have the same menu of potential shots the tour player has at his or her disposal, but there's no reason you can't visualize *your* menu of shots just as well. And your ability to visualize what *you* want to do next dramatically increases your chances of actually doing it.

As we discussed in Chapter Six, you can produce this preview image of your shot in your mind in primarily a visual way or primarily a feel-related way. If you're visually oriented, you get behind the ball and follow it in its imagined flight. If you're more feel oriented, you use this kinesthetic sense. I've heard Tiger Woods describe how he hits a draw: by feeling the sensation of the back of his left hand squaring to the target a couple of inches before impact.

Either way you do it, you're engaging the right/creative side of your brain and priming the neural passageways for what comes next.

Case Study

I was in Arizona to see a client at the Tucson PGA Tour event years ago, and we decided to walk and talk together during his Tuesday practice round. He played that day with a guy who hadn't yet secured full playing privileges on tour but had gotten some attention for some high finishes overseas. I spent the first nine or ten holes talking to my client, then drifted off to the side for a bit to let him think about some of the things

PRE-SHOT PYRAMID

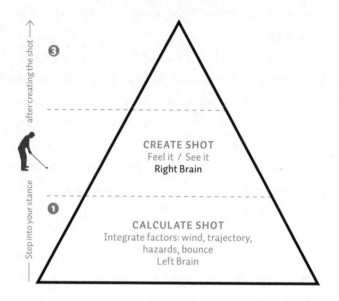

after creating the shot →

❸

CREATE SHOT
Feel it / See it
Right Brain

Step into your stance

❶

CALCULATE SHOT
Integrate factors: wind, trajectory,
hazards, bounce
Left Brain

we were working on. This gave me an opportunity to study the other player, who had a very unorthodox pre-shot routine.

After getting to his ball, he would talk to his caddie for a minute, pull a club, and then take a few quick practice swings. But at least half of the time he would get to his ball, change his mind, and then go back for another club. This process would sometimes repeat itself three or four times before he actually pulled the trigger on his shot.

At first I couldn't figure out if this was all a part of an elaborate pre-shot routine—one he went through so that he could feel comfortable over a shot. But after a few holes I could see that he only went through that indecisive ritual when he had a challenging shot. On a wide-open par-5, he got up and ripped it without hesitation—and the same was true for most of his putts.

I don't offer unsolicited advice to players, but when we finished the practice round, this player came over to me and described exactly what I had been seeing: that on difficult shots he had trouble picturing what he wanted to do. That issue was compounded by the fact that he was a tremendously gifted ball striker. He had a lot of options to choose from, and when he was presented with a shot that offered him those choices, he struggled to pick one.

He asked me for advice about how to simplify the process. He said he wasn't standing over his shots with a complete, committed picture of what he wanted to do. Plus he was sensitive to the fact that his indecisive routine was taking a lot of time—and potentially annoying his playing partners.

I asked him what he did to picture the shot in his head before hitting it, and he paused for a few seconds. He said he thought about it as if he were watching a highlight of himself on television hitting it—the swing, and then a cutaway to the ball landing on the grass.

I told him that the only way to judge his method was whether or not it was working for him—and obviously it wasn't. I suggested that he play a round where he went with the first shot that came to his mind when getting to his ball. He was talented enough to hit *all* of them and just needed to see and commit to one. I then suggested that he simplify things so that he simply pictured the flight of the ball as if he were watching it on high-definition television from its flight to its landing spot and eventually to where it ended up.

He thanked me and shook my hand, and we went our separate ways.

The next time I saw him, he was on television and in contention Sunday afternoon a few weeks later. I watched him go through his process with his caddie, and after he picked his club he closed his eyes for few seconds to see his shot. He walked into his stance, took one look at the target, and hit the shot.

He ended up winning that week, and has been a consistent performer for the last decade.

I still get a very nice Christmas card from him and his family, even though our professional relationship only lasted ten minutes!

STEP THREE: EXECUTE

First, you figured out what shot you wanted to hit and selected your club. Next, you created a preview of the shot in your mind.

Now it's time to hit the shot.

What should you think about now?

I've had thousands of conversations with elite athletes over the last thirty years, and virtually all of them offered strikingly similar descriptions of their mental state when they were in The Zone—and competing at their best. Whether it was Eric Heiden talking about speed skating in our organic chemistry class at Stanford or John McEnroe describing what it felt like to beat Björn Borg in the 1981 Wimbledon final, almost everyone has told me that within that zone of peak performance they aren't thinking about much at all.

"Mindless" doesn't have quite the right connotation for that place, so I came up with the term "know mind"—a place of awareness and execution with no focus on specific physical movements.

When I talk about The Zone, or this "know mind" space, many people ask me if it's anything like hypnotism. Honestly, it *is* a form of self-hypnotism, but I don't like to use that word because of the potential negative connotations. It isn't hypnotism like you see in the movies, where a person goes under and starts quacking like a duck.

In the true scientific sense, hypnotism is focused attention with the suspension of external stimuli. In other words, you're concentrating on one thing to the point where you don't notice what's going on around you. You can think of your focus level as being on a scale. At one end you're fully hypnotized, and on the other you're completely distracted. The Zone and the "know mind" state are on the more focused half of that scale. The tool for moving your level of concentration in the right direction is the Pre-Shot Pyramid. You're creating a trigger system to help put you in that more focused state.

There's no question that the ability to put yourself in that Zen-like place at will is a special one that most people never achieve. In fact, I believe it's one of the main qualities that separates the very top tier of athletes from "run of the mill" professionals. People like Eric Heiden, John McEnroe, Tiger Woods, and Michael Jordan clearly have a gift.

Before you get discouraged about not having this "magic" switch, I have some good news.

You can get to the "know mind" state—or at least a reasonable approximation of it—through a mental trapdoor.

Our brains are wired to be constantly processing information—from the five senses and from memory, consciously and unconsciously. It's a defense mechanism honed over millions of years. But one thing our minds can't do is consciously process more than one thought at a time.

If you can't make your mind go quiet—which is hard to do—you can instead *substitute* a productive thought you choose for the one that's in your head now. *Thought substitution* is one of the most valuable tools in your arsenal, and a huge help as you make your way through the Pre-Shot Pyramid.

Legendary Hall of Famer Billy Casper used thought substitution long before any "expert" told him how well it would work. He described for me how he would walk onto the tee of a tight, treacherous par-4 and instead of thinking about how hard the next shot was going to be, he'd fill his mind with a calming phrase in a loop like "Nice and easy" or "Finish high." That would replace a thought like "Stay right, away from the water" or "Don't hook it."

You can use any nonspecific calming phrase you like, as long as it stays away from the province managed by your technical left brain. For example, you wouldn't want to use thoughts like "Fire my right side" or "Turn my shoulders past parallel."

By substituting a calm, neutral thought for a stressful or technical one, you're pushing your mind into a still, quiet place when it's time for action. Then you can swing freely and instinctively.

You don't even need a negative thought in your head for this concept to work. You can preprogram your mind with an "anchor" thought ahead of time so that it's occupying space and preventing a negative or unproductive thought from entering. The anchor thought can be the same one you'd use in thought substitution. You're just using it sooner.

Former NFL placekicker Nate Kaeding was a long-time client, and he and I initially met on the golf course. We got to talking about how similar placekicking was to golf. In both sports, you get the chance to initiate the action. You aren't constrained by the fluid activities of a bunch of other people around you, like you would be in soccer or even other positions on the football field.

I demonstrated to Nate many of the same mental techniques I'd used with golfers. Namely, we worked on the idea of using an anchor thought as he approached each kick. Using that technique, he set an NFL record for consecutive kicks converted from less than fifty yards. In times when he struggled, we also borrowed directly from Billy Casper and his thought-substitution pattern. Nate's common miss was a hook, and instead of obsessing about that or thinking about the consequences of missing the kick, he substituted the simple, nontechnical thought "Finish high." It was especially useful considering that a high finish with his leg would make it almost impossible for him to hit a hook.

PRE-SHOT PYRAMID

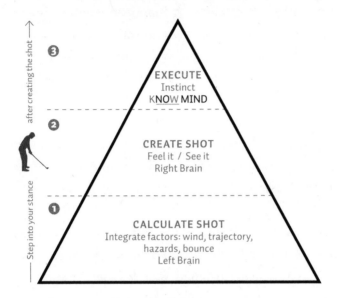

Case Study

As I described in the Introduction, watching some-body like Phil Mickelson practice is a special experience. The great players in any sport are like Mozart, doing things you almost can't believe would be possible.

But the simple reality of having that kind of skill can sometimes cause these players some interesting problems.

Just before the Masters in 2012, I was in a small

group of people standing on the practice green Phil has at his house, watching him experiment with a variety of different putters and putting styles. He was alternating between his normal putter and normal style and other variations with a belly putter and different kinds of grips.

Phil made his way around the practice green, rolling short putts and long putts with the different clubs and styles, trying to parse out which one he would use at the Masters.

He asked me what I thought, and I told him I would leave the technical discussions to guys like Dave Stockton and Butch Harmon; but from a mental perspective, which particular style he used was less important than picking one style. He needed to go with one and then stop thinking about it.

The reality is that competition burns energy. That's just as true at the Masters as it is when you're playing your buddies for $5. You need all of your energy and focus to deal with the stress of competing, and you don't want to burn it on thinking about mechanics—even if you're able to "forget" the mechanical part when you're over the ball.

Over the next few months Phil and I worked on "forgetting" everything. When he was practicing, the questions were "Does it feel comfortable?" and "Does it match what the instructor wants me to do?" If so, go with it.

One of Phil's great gifts—among many—is the ability to understand what element of his game needs work and to compartmentalize his work on just that part of the game. If he doesn't feel good about his putting, or his mental game, or his long game, he's able to accurately diagnose the problem and make a rational decision to work on that element—without trashing everything else.

That's exactly what he did in this case. He metabolized the concept of playing "naturally" and got away from thinking about three different kinds of putting strokes, or different swings with his driver and the rest of his clubs. He's one of the few guys talented enough to actually consider those things, but they weren't making his job easier.

Phil has been able to simplify his thought process and play without getting "clogged." This has made the process of identifying the physical things to work on with his instructors much more straightforward.

ONCE YOU'VE ASSEMBLED the pieces of the Pre-Shot Pyramid into a productive, efficient, and consistent routine, you're ready to hit great shots. Before we move on and discuss the measurement tool you'll use to gauge your progress on that front, let's take a final exam to make sure you've mastered the building-block concepts.

EXAM

Evaluate the following visualization descriptions actual tour players have used in their pre-shot routines. Which ones are vision based and which are feel based?

STATEMENT 1

Before a putt, the path the ball is going to take on the green stands out as a red line. I see the spot where the ball is going to enter the hole as a number on a clockface.

[visual]   [feel]

STATEMENT 2

All I'm trying to do is keep the back of my left wrist going down the target line as long as I can.

[visual]   [feel]

STATEMENT 3

When I need to hit it long, I'm trying to create creases in the right leg of my pants.

[visual]   [feel]

STATEMENT 4

I'll line up my shot with a leaf or something on the ground a few inches ahead of my ball and something in the distance behind my target. Then I'll trace a shot that covers both lines.

[visual]   [feel]

STATEMENT 5

With the driver, I feel like I'm standing on one rail of the train tracks and the ball is on the other rail. I'm swinging on my rail and the ball goes down the other rail.

[visual]   [feel]

STATEMENT 6

When the pressure is on, I'm thinking about more body turn and dead arms for lower, less spinning shots.

[visual]   [feel]

Answers

Statement 1: visual
Statement 2: feel
Statement 3: feel
Statement 4: visual
Statement 5: visual
Statement 6: feel

Which of the six thoughts below are candidates for thought substitution?

Statement 1: Left is dead here.
Statement 2: Finish my backswing.
Statement 3: Just hit it on the green.
Statement 4: Crush it.
Statement 5: The hole is so tight, a bogey is a good score here.
Statement 6: Take the club more inside.

Answers

Statement 1: Substitute for negative thought: Target area is mower stripe on right side of fairway.
Statement 2: Acceptable.

Statement 3: Substitute. Pick a more specific
  target, then use a generic, positive thought.

Statement 4: Acceptable.

Statement 5: Substitute for negative thought:
  Use an iron off the tee here.

Statement 6: Substitute. Technical thought
  gets in the way of instinctive swing.

CHAPTER 9

The Mental Scorecard System

A T ITS CORE, golf seems to be a results-oriented game.

There's a scorecard and a pencil, and you're judging yourself (or being judged) by the numbers you write in the boxes.

Those numbers get combined to make birdies, bogeys, and pars, and tournament scores, match results, and handicaps—all results we use to measure our games and ourselves. Amateurs are categorized by their handicaps, and tour players are categorized by wins and money.

That's about as results oriented as you can get.

Given that most of us are intensely results-oriented people, you would think this results orientation in golf would be a productive thing.

But the cruel irony is that results orientation *hinders* your performance when you're on the golf course. As we talked about in Chapter Two, results orientation is fine for practice, when you're trying to learn a new skill. But when you're trying to perform your best when it counts, *process orientation* is a much more effective approach.

Of course, that presents the fundamental question we're trying to answer in this book. *In a results-oriented game and with a results-oriented mind, how do you play process-oriented golf out on the course?*

You do it with the Mental Scorecard.

You know how to use a standard scorecard to keep your conventional score. Each hole you play has a designated par, and you write down the number of swings you took to play the hole. You can be below par, at par, or above par.

But with the Mental Scorecard system, I'm not concerned with the number of shots you take to play a hole. Instead, you rate the quality of your mental approach on each shot you hit.

Ideally, you get immersed in the quest to successfully implement each mental element. By rating yourself on how you do, you're satisfying the need for results-oriented feedback, but you're doing it in a way that works toward the greater goal of being process oriented as you play.

You get to have it both ways!

The foundation of the Mental Scorecard is the Pre-Shot Pyramid and the three-step routine outlined in the last chapter. For each shot you take, your goal is to successfully negotiate the three steps of the Pyramid in order. If you're able to complete all three steps, you earn one point for that shot. If you don't complete one or more of the steps for that shot, you earn zero points.

PRE-SHOT PYRAMID

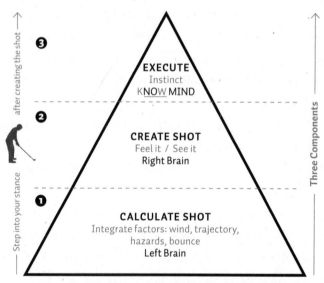

after creating the shot →

❸

EXECUTE
Instinct
K<u>NOW</u> MIND

❷

CREATE SHOT
Feel it / See it
Right Brain

Step into your stance

❶

CALCULATE SHOT
Integrate factors: wind, trajectory,
hazards, bounce
Left Brain

Three Components

Player must implement ALL THREE mental skills per shot in
order for the shot to qualify and to get a 1/1 score.
(Goal is to have 100 percent of shots all receiving a point.)

At the end of the round, you'll have a mental score that works in tandem with the standard score you record. Your mental score will be a fraction of one hundred, with 100 percent being perfect. If you executed your three-step process successfully on seventy-five out of ninety shots, you would have a mental score of 83 percent (75/90 = 83 percent).

It's important to note that your grade for executing your mental process successfully is independent of the shot's actual result. You could hit your approach shot to ten feet and convert the putt for birdie, but if you go back and notice that you failed to fully visualize the shot (step two), you wouldn't get a point for that shot. Conversely, you would get a point on the Mental Scorecard if you went through your complete process and hit a grounder off the tee. Another important point to note is that penalty shots count under the original swing you made. For example, if you hit a tee shot out of bounds but go through your complete routine as planned, you would score yourself 2 for 2 on the Mental Scorecard—one for the swing and one for the penalty shot. Conversely, if your routine was bad, you would score yourself 0 for 2. This keeps the scorekeeping clean and in line with your real score.

Let me take you through a stretch of four sample holes to give you a nuts-and-bolts look at how to fill the scorecard out. The 1st hole is a 407-yard par-4. You

DR. MICHAEL T. LARDON

hit a mediocre tee shot in the fairway but far from the hole. You have two hundred yards in, and you hit a hybrid up into the first cut of rough just left and short. After a decent chip, you two-putt for bogey.

As you make your way to the 2nd tee, you replay the five shots in your mind. You realize that you didn't take the necessary time to factor in wind conditions and pick the ideal target on your second shot. You basically just pulled a hybrid with the thought that you were going to blast it up by the green somewhere and hope for the best. On the other four shots, you went through your full, correct three-stop Pre-Shot Pyramid.

So your mental score for the 1st hole would be 4/5—four successful shots out of five.

On the 2nd hole, a 523-yard par-5, you hit a great tee shot up the left side of the fairway to set up a great angle to the widest part of the second-shot landing area. After a good hybrid shot to the ideal layup area, you hit a nice 8-iron to fifteen feet and make the putt for birdie.

As you walk to the next tee, you replay the four shots in your mind—filtering out the understandable excitement that comes from making birdie—and note that you went through your full and complete routine on all four shots.

Your score for the 2nd hole is 4/4.

On the 3rd hole, a 410-yard par-4, you're feeling pumped up because you just made the birdie, plus the

3rd is your favorite hole on the course. You go through your process and make the conscious decision to use driver even though the fairway cuts in at your landing area. You end up forty feet short of the hole, with a tough double-breaking putt. You go through your full, complete routine for each putt, and get down in two.

Your score for the 3rd hole is 4/4. You hit it into the rough, and end up 60 feet away after your approach shot.

On the 4th hole, a 348-yard par-4, you walk onto the tee still thinking about the good two-putt on the last hole, and you rush your routine. You don't make a swing with a clear, neutral mind and you pull it into the first cut on the left. You then hit an indifferent shot onto the green. Two putts later, you hole out for a boring par. Overall, it was a sloppy result on a birdie-able hole. You only completed your full routine on the first putt.

Your score for the 4th hole is 1/4—even though you made par.

Based on our simulated stretch of holes, your total real score was 17, while you scored 13 out of 17 on the Mental Scorecard. By taking the shots where you qualified by completing the Pre-Shot Pyramid (Q) and dividing them by the number of real shots you took (R), you get your mental score:

$$Q/R = 13/17 = 76 \text{ percent}$$

MENTAL SCORECARD SYSTEM
(sample score for just 9 holes)

HOLE	1	2	3	4	5	6	7	8	9		Q/R	%
PAR	4	5	4	4	3	4	5	3	4	36		
NUMBER OF SHOTS THAT QUALIFY (Q)	4	4	4	1	13							
REAL SCORE (R)	5	4	4	4	17					76%		
OVERALL % FRACTION Q/R	4/5	4/4	4/4	1/4	13/17							

The Q signifies both the fact that the shot qualified and that it was a quality shot.

I've tracked thousands of golfers over the years, and I've found that a good mental score correlates to a good real score at least 85 percent of the time—and more than 90 percent of the time for PGA Tour players and high-level amateurs. If you can consistently improve your mental score average, you will see a parallel improvement in your handicap. Just remember that individual scores on either card are data points.

Don't let the data points overwhelm you. Focus on the overall trends and where you're headed.

When I share this Mental Scorecard system with someone—whether it's a tour player or a 10-handicapper—one of the first questions I get is "What is a good score?"

It depends.

The very best tour players score 98 or 99 percent on this card. Phil Mickelson will talk about being right mentally on all but one or two shots in a given round. I've worked with Lee Janzen for years, and he isn't happy if his score is below 95 percent.

As you work your way down the golf food chain, the percentages decrease. A top 100 player on the PGA Tour should consistently be above 90 percent. Most of the Web.com Tour players I work with are in the 85 percent range when they start. Good college players are usually in the low 80s. Single-digit amateur players usually score in the 60s.

At the tour level, the difference between winning a major championship and keeping your playing privileges is seven or eight percentage points—five or six shots per round with less than full concentration, which results in about a one-shot difference in scoring average. It shows you just how tightly bunched the players are at the game's top tier and what an achievement it is for the great players to separate themselves.

Tour players need every mental advantage they can find just to survive. Amateur players can see huge improvements just by making rudimentary changes in their mental approach.

If you're an 18-handicap who's never paid any attention to your mental process and you started from scratch after reading this book, I'd expect you to be able to score somewhere in the 30 to 40 percent range for your first few rounds.

But just by paying attention and *trying* instead of checking out from time to time, you'll quickly be able to improve into the 60 percent range. For an 18-handicap, that's the difference between shooting 85 and 93—all without making a single mechanical change.

Case Study

A few years ago, an amateur golfer from Texas saw an article about me and David Duval in a magazine and called to see if we could work together. Scott Fawcett and I hit it off right away, and we quickly established where he could find the most improvement. Scott struggled with getting too technical in his thoughts before swinging and needed a way to clear his mind. I set him up with the Pre-Shot Pyramid and the Mental Scorecard, along with some exercises designed specifically for his issue.

Scott is a self-described "Excel nerd," and he embraced the concept of keeping a Mental Scorecard with great enthusiasm. The first season he used it, he tracked his performance religiously and immersed himself in the "game" aspect of it. How much improvement could he see over the course of a summer?

At the beginning of the season, Scott played in the Texas Amateur and recorded a mental score of 81 percent. Digging into the numbers, he realized that he hadn't used his full focus on 52 out of the 280 shots he hit during that tournament. That just steeled his resolve.

As Scott progressed through the summer, his average mental score percentage edged into the high 80s. He entered the U.S. Mid-Amateur and went out in 29 over the first nine holes of the match play qualifying round. He told me that he was so engrossed with the Mental Scorecard that night that he didn't even realize he was 7 under at the turn until his playing partner mentioned it on the 10th hole. He ended up shooting 66 that day and qualified for the match play portion of the event.

At the end of the summer, Scott decided to give PGA Tour Q-school a try just to satisfy his curiosity about how well he could really play. He made it through the prequalifying tournament, then shot four rounds in the 60s to make it through the first stage. After a 12th-place finish at the second stage tournament in Brooksville, Florida, Scott made the final field of 163 in Q-school finals in La Quinta, California. There, he shot a combined score of 426—6 under par—to earn a provisional card on the Web.com Tour for the next season.

When Scott compiled his Mental Scorecard statistics after the six rounds of Q-school finals, he found that he had made it to 92 percent. When he was finished, he told me that he felt like if he had made it to 95 percent, he could have earned a card on the PGA Tour. That would have meant going through his process completely on 12 more shots over the course of six rounds.

All of this success came in a year when, at the beginning of it, Scott didn't even win his own club championship. At the start of the season, he was a plus-4 handicap. By the end, he was a plus-6.5—an incredible improvement for a player with a handicap that low. A two-and-half-shot difference on the PGA Tour for a full season is the difference between playing in the Tour Championship with the other top 30 players and finishing outside the top 150 and losing your card.

Scott said the biggest bonus the Mental Scorecard offered him—in addition to letting him redirect his focus from technical thoughts—was that it allowed him to acknowledge his anxiety and stress and then have a mechanism for letting it go. To that end, he wrote "Acknowledge" on the side of his ball when he played in the qualifying events—something he still does to this day.

Scott runs a thriving electrical supply business in Dallas, so it wasn't as simple as dropping everything to go play Web.com events in 2009. His status got him into one early-season event where he opened with rounds of 68 to 66 before struggling. After the reshuffle, he would have had to play lots of Monday qualifying rounds to get in, so he was content to go back to his previous life with most of his questions answered.

Scott showed himself he could play at the professional level.

I'M CERTAINLY THRILLED that Scott's performance validated the Pre-Shot Pyramid and Mental Scorecard in such a dramatic way, but the fact that he earned a Web.com Tour spot isn't the biggest part of the story as far as how this all relates to the average player. After all, Scott is an exceptionally talented guy—a former Division I scholarship golfer at Texas A&M.

No, my favorite part of the story is what Scott had to say about the mental processes he learned as they applied to the customer golf he now plays as a businessman.

I'll let him tell the story:

By working on the building blocks, I dropped two and a half strokes per round. To portray that to a 20-handicap, that would probably equate to going from 25 percent on the Mental Scorecard to 50 percent. That's the difference between being a 20-handicapper and a 12-handicapper—just by paying more attention on forty-five of the ninety shots you play.

That isn't a guess. When I go out and play with customers and they're struggling, I make them an offer. I say, "Just trust me and do what I tell you to in terms of thinking through what you're going to do and changing your strategy." I'm showing them how to think the way Doc Lardon taught me. Without exception, they've played the best golf of their life.

Homework

For the next month, incorporate the Mental Scorecard system into your playing routine and keep it in tandem with your regular score. You can do it on a second scorecard from the course you're playing, or at the bottom of your regular card. At the end of the month, compare your overall USGA handicap to what it was thirty days before. Compare this to the trend in your mental score averages. How are both numbers tracking?

The Mental Scorecard works because it organizes your mental energy most efficiently. And that effect increases the longer you use it. Every time you record your mental score—regardless of how well you do— you're taking steps toward automating your pre-shot routine. As your pre-shot routine becomes automated, you'll gradually stop thinking about each of the steps as individual pieces. They'll happen naturally, in sequence. This familiarization and automation is what leads to "mental toughness"—the ability to continue with your routine and mental processes regardless of the situation.

Your confidence and toughness will start to develop because the Mental Scorecard routine gives you a sense of control. You're no longer at the complete mercy of random thoughts and anxiety when you play. It doesn't mean those thoughts and feelings disappear. You've just developed the ability to recognize and channel them in a productive way. By practicing concentration, you're improving your ability to have it when you need it.

MENTAL SCORECARD SYSTEM
(blank 9-hole sample scorecard)

HOLE	1	2	3	4	5	6	7	8	9		Q/R	%
PAR												
NUMBER OF SHOTS THAT QUALIFY (Q)												
REAL SCORE (R)												
OVERALL % FRACTION Q/R												

When I describe the Pre-Shot Pyramid to my tour clients, they almost always ask me what percentage other tour players are reaching—again, a sign of that results orientation we've been talking about. When I tell them the number is around 95 percent, they usually say something to the effect that they think they could get to that number as well.

My response usually throws them off. I say, "If your child's life was dependent on you meticulously going through these three steps as you hit every shot, what percentage would you score?"

Given that set of parameters, they instantly say they could score 100 percent.

I follow that response with the logical extension.

"If you think you could record a score of 100 percent under those conditions, then a perfect mental round is possible, right?"

Like Roger Bannister's sub-four-minute mile, the realization that a 100 percent round is possible changes the bar in terms of setting goals. The encouraging thing about this goal—or any other percentage goal with the Mental Scorecard—is that it can be achieved with effort. Regardless of past thoughts or future results, you can stay in the moment and be in full control of everything that happens up to the moment of contact with the ball.

Control breeds confidence, and confidence breeds good play.

Used correctly, the Mental Scorecard operates like an additional set of gauges in your car. The speedometer can tell you how fast you're going, but the other gauges give you different information that is just as important, like engine temperature and fuel level.

Having this additional gauge gives you much more precision in how you evaluate your game. It's essentially a tachometer that measures the quality of your mental focus. Nobody plays well every round—not even tour players. Some days your swing mechanics are to blame, while other days you might not be thinking as well as you could be. Most days it's a mixture of those two factors.

But without some way of analyzing your mental performance, you're likely to walk off the course with a blanket attitude of "I played bad" without any insight into exactly why—or, worse yet, a mistaken conclusion. You're sabotaging your game and undermining your confidence by attributing a bad score to a swing problem when the cause might actually be something else, like a lack of concentration.

With good information you can come off the course and immediately say, "My swing is out of whack, but I thought my way around the course well," or vice versa. You have some direction for what you need to work on plus the basis for feeling good about one part of your game.

And giving yourself some affirmation and credit for the things you're doing well is a crucial part of this equation. Establishing in your mind that you've been successful at your three-part Pre-Shot Pyramid time after time leads you to know that you can do it again successfully. It also helps you "own" all of the shots you hit. If you go through your preparations properly and completely, you've done all you can do. You're free to embrace the results when they're positive and accept them when they're less than positive.

I can give you a great example of this from a sport that has surprising similarities to golf. In show jumping, a rider pilots a horse around a complex course with a series of barriers of different heights. The rider's score is determined by how long it takes him or her to navigate the course, with penalties for each barrier that gets knocked over in the process.

Vinton Karrasch came to me to see if I could help him translate his strong performances in practice to the competition field—something that should be familiar to every golfer. Much like golf, show jumping is a mix of mental and physical challenges. Both sports are scored on precision and avoiding critical mistakes.

Vinton struggled because he viewed his competitive goal in terms of what he needed to do to execute a perfect run. He approached every event with the thought that he needed to be great to have a chance to win. Using an adapted version of the Mental Scorecard, we worked on adjusting his focus so that he was more interested in what he needed to be doing with his horse at a given time through each run—the process—than about some nebulous concept of being "great" overall.

If Vinton followed his script and put his horse into position at each barrier, the results would take care of themselves. If he did this to the best of his ability, he would be able to accept the results, whatever they were.

This idea of process orientation and ownership liberated Vinton to approach competitions with a completely different attitude. Instead of second-guessing his preparation and holding on to the fear of making a killer mistake, he went in knowing he had the tools to do the best he could do. It paid off too. Vinton and his horse Coral Reef Baloufino won their first grand prix event, the Rancho Valencia World Cup Grand Prix of Del Mar, in 2013. Now he's aiming for a spot on the 2016 U.S. Olympic team.

One of the great side effects of embracing the Mental Scorecard is this sense of acceptance and ownership of what you do out on the course, whether it's a golf course, a show jumping course, a ski slope, a football field, or any other arena. You're able to "metabolize" in a healthier, more efficient way, allowing you to learn and move past a bad result.

That resilience is incredibly useful in a game as potentially frustrating as golf.

Case Study

Not many people would have picked Paul Goydos in a head-to-head matchup against Sergio García in a playoff at the 2008 Players Championship. Goydos was a forty-three-year-old journeyman with two wins in fifteen years on the PGA Tour, and García had twenty-five wins in his ten years as a professional.

But Goydos had played well all week, and came into the final round with a one-shot lead over Kenny Perry and a three-shot advantage over García. After some stumbles, he made clutch pars on 17 and 18 to preserve his chance to earn the biggest win of his career in the playoff with García.

But it wasn't to be. On the first sudden-death playoff hole, on the treacherous 120-yard island 17th, Goydos hit his tee shot into the water.

Many players—especially ones who, like Goydos, were closer to the end of their career than the beginning—would have been devastated by the loss. But Goydos came into the media center in an upbeat mood and said he had no regrets about his performance. He said that he hit a similar shot thirty minutes before, in regulation, and it went right where he planned. In the playoff, he went through his routine just the way he wanted and hit the exact shot he saw in his mind, but a gust of wind took the ball into the water.

Keeping great perspective, Goydos said that he hit a good shot and played well all week, but García played a little bit better. He said he felt like he had controlled all the variables he could control. Some he couldn't, and that's just the way it went. He didn't let the bad luck of an ill-timed gust of wind ruin the experience of playing great and having a clean Mental Scorecard when it counted.

Two years later, Goydos became only the fourth player in PGA Tour history to shoot 59 in a round when he made twelve birdies and six pars in the first round of the John Deere Classic.

ONCE YOU'VE DIGESTED the basics—the Six Components of Mental Excellence, the Pre-Shot Pyramid, and the Mental Scorecard—it's natural to wonder how long it will take to see real improvement in your on-course results.

The human brain loves novelty. It gets the dopamine flowing. When you present your mind with these new tools, I'm sure you're going to see a "honeymoon" period like the one Scott Fawcett described earlier in this chapter.

What you do next, once the honeymoon is over,

will determine how far the Mental Scorecard will take you.

After a month or so, you'll reach the point where you either consolidate the improvements you've made to your thinking pattern and routine and fully integrate them into your game, or you will give up and go back to what's comfortable. Bad habits can return with a vengeance if you aren't vigilant about what you're doing. Bad habits are broken by developing good ones.

The second phase is where you put in the work—the shoe leather, so to speak—to grind it out and make these techniques an automatic part of your game. For most players this begins to happen after about twenty rounds using the Mental Scorecard. For a tour player, that means about three weeks of work. If you're a weekend player who doesn't practice much in between, it might take you the entire summer.

Get through this second phase and you're going to see new, permanent improvements to your game. You'll be the mentally tough golfer you've always wanted to be.

When that happens for you, I want to hear your story. E-mail me through my Web site, DrLardon.com. I'll post the best responses to inspire other golfers just like you.

Afterword

WHEN A TOUR player with the ambition to become the best in the world hires me to help, it might seem like a daunting task—for both of us. That's a tall mountain to climb in any discipline, whether it's golf or life. But that job is no more daunting than my four-year-old son Theo's burning aspiration.

He wants to fly a rocket to the moon.

Every night before bed, we watch video clips of Neil Armstrong's first step on the lunar surface in 1969. In Theo's mind, he has no doubt he'll accomplish the same feat someday. So when we finish building one of our model rockets together, he's never satisfied with the results.

"It's too small, Daddy," he says. "We can never fit inside."

He really wants to build a full-size rocket so he can make that trip, and he knows it's possible because he's seen somebody do it. He's watched Armstrong and Buzz Aldrin go up in *Apollo 11* a hundred times.

Whatever your goals are for your own game, Theo's rocket metaphor applies to you too.

To get to the moon, you have to follow a deliberate process. You need to train as an astronaut, and the spaceship has to be designed and built. Once it's launched, it needs to travel in the right direction, and it needs sufficient fuel. It needs to be strong enough to reach the destination and sturdy enough to stand up to the heat of reentry.

In golf, you need a deliberate plan for improvement. You have to train your body and mind to get there. Your improvement plan needs to have the right direction, and you need the right motivational fuel. You need to have the mental fortitude to stand up to the rigors of competition—to survive when the heat is on.

When you apply your skills in a disciplined way every day, you draw a tight focus on your goal. The moon doesn't look so far away anymore. Winning your major championship becomes very possible.

Keep that passion and self-belief and continue to enjoy yourself in this great game, and anything is possible!

I hope *Mastering Golf's Mental Game* has become the reference guide you need to keep yourself on track for this great journey. Mark the pages that mean the most to you and tuck the book into your bag for a quick tune-up when you're on the practice range or getting ready to tee off. You can also visit my Web site for more tips and techniques and extra motivation.

I know some of the work we've done together has been difficult, and I know you'll feel some frustration from time to time. But like Dr. Schawlow said to me all those years ago in physics class: If you want to truly be good at something, you're going to feel some pain. It's going to hurt, but it's the good kind of hurt—and it's worth the effort.

I hope to see you on the links!

Dr. Michael Lardon
San Diego, California
January 25, 2014
DrLardon.com

Acknowledgments

I am grateful to many people for their insight, inspiration, and guidance throughout the process of creating this book. I would like to dedicate this book first and foremost to my wife, Nadine, and my children, Lexi, Lindsay, and Theo, who spent too many weekends watching Dad type away at the computer instead of taking them to Legoland.

I want to thank my writer, Matthew Rudy, whose quiet ease and effortless skill made this project a true pleasure to complete. Farley Chase, my agent, inspired me to start working on this book in earnest with a phone call several years after we worked together on *Finding Your Zone*, and he once again provided me with invaluable guidance and support. I also want to thank Dominick Anfuso at Crown Archetype, whose passion for golf and belief in my work led to what I hope is a valuable, readable guide, for any golfer. I'm also grateful to Professor Tim Boggan, who has encouraged my writing throughout my life and who provided invaluable feedback that shaped the contents of this book. Special thanks go to my illustrator, Brian Chojnowski.

Many people helped me in ways that they may not know: my father, Robert Lardon; my mother, Barbara Lardon; my brother, Brad Lardon; my sister-in-law, Sabine Lardon; and my dear friend and collaborator, Michelle Fitzpatrick. I also want to thank Perry Schwartzberg, Michael Fitzgerald, Jamie Thomas, George Wurzer, Scot Morris, Tom Strong, Dave Watt, Josh Algra, Eric Heiden, John Polich, Bob Niculescu, Richard Bunt, Rocco Fabiano, Andy Chou, Jon Schulberg, Marty Bauer, and Stellan Bengtsson, and my assistants, Chris Oyas, Edith Mendoza, and Dr. Barb Edwards. From the golf world, I want to thank David and Kelly Leadbetter, Rick Schloss, Freddie Jacobson, Rich Beem, David Duval, Steve Marino, Charles Howell III, Lee Janzen, John Mallinger, Erik Compton, Scott Fawcett, Billy Heim, Puggy Blackmon, Chris Riley, Billy Casper, and Phil Mickelson.

And to all the golfers—tour players and duffers alike—this book is for you. We all love this game, with all of its charms and frustrations. It generates a passion unlike anything else. By sharing these mental fundamentals, I hope you shoot lower scores, but more importantly, I hope you get more enjoyment out of the game.

Reading List

Baron, David A., Claudia L. Reardon, and Steven H. Baron, eds., *Clinical Sports Psychiatry: An International Perspective.* West Sussex, UK: Wiley-Blackwell, 2013.

Coyle, Daniel. *The Talent Code: Greatness Isn't Born. It's Grown. Here's How.* New York: Bantam, 2009.

Csikszentmihalyi, Mihaly. *Flow: The Psychology of Optimal Experience.* New York, Harper & Row, 1990.

Epstein, David. *The Sports Gene: Inside the Science of Extraordinary Athletic Performance.* New York: Current, 2013.

Gallwey, W. Timothy. *The Inner Game of Tennis: The Classic Guide to the Mental Side of Peak Performance.* New York: Random House, 1997.

Kotler, Steven. *The Rise of Superman: Decoding the Science of Ultimate Human Performance.* New York: Houghton Mifflin Harcourt, 2014.

Lardon, Michael. *Finding Your Zone: Ten Core Lessons for*

Achieving Peak Performance in Sports and Life. New York: Perigee Trade, 2008.

Luttrell, Marcus, with Patrick Robinson. *Lone Survivor: The Eyewitness Account of Operation Redwing and the Lost Heroes of SEAL Team 10*. New York: Little, Brown and Company, 2013.

Orlick, Terry. *In Pursuit of Excellence*, 4th ed. Champaign, IL: Human Kinetics, 2007.

Parent, Joseph. *Zen Golf: Mastering the Mental Game*. New York: Doubleday, 2002.

Penick, Harvey. *Harvey Penick's Little Red Book: Lessons and Teachings from a Lifetime in Golf*. New York: Simon & Schuster, 1992.

Rotella, Bob. *Golf Is Not a Game of Perfect*. New York: Simon and Schuster, 1995.

Stockton, Dave, with Matthew Rudy. *Unconscious Putting: Dave Stockton's Guide to Unlocking Your Signature Stroke*. New York: Gotham, 2011.

Utley, Stan, with Matthew Rudy. *The Art of Putting: The Revolutionary Feel-Based System for Improving Your Score*. New York: Gotham, 2006.